CASEMIRO

MATT & TOM OLDFIELD

ULTIMATE
FOOTBALL HEROES

CASEMIRO

FROM THE PLAYGROUND
TO THE PITCH

DINO

First published by Dino Books in 2023,
an imprint of Bonnier Books UK,
4th Floor, Victoria House, Bloomsbury Square, London WC1B 4DA
Owned by Bonnier Books,
Sveavägen 56, Stockholm, Sweden

𝕏 @UFHbooks
𝕏 @footieheroesbks
www.heroesfootball.com
www.bonnierbooks.co.uk

Text © Studio Press 2023

Design by www.envydesign.co.uk

All rights reserved. No part of this publication may be reproduced, stored in a
retrieval system, or transmitted in any form or by any means, without the prior
permission in writing of the publisher, nor be otherwise circulated in any form
of binding or cover other than that in which it is published and without a similar
condition including this condition being imposed on the subsequent purchaser.

Paperback ISBN: 978 1 78946 490 0
E-book ISBN: 978 1 78946 498 6

British Library cataloguing-in-publication data:
A catalogue record for this book is available from the British Library.

Printed and bound in Great Britain by Clays Ltd, Elcograf S.p.A.

3 5 7 9 10 8 6 4

All names and trademarks are the property of their respective owners,
which are in no way associated with Dino Books. Use of these
names does not imply any cooperation or endorsement.

For all readers,
young and old(er)

ULTIMATE
FOOTBALL HEROES

Matt Oldfield is a children's author focusing on the wonderful world of football. His other books include *Unbelievable Football* (winner of the 2020 Children's Sports Book of the Year) and the *Johnny Ball: Football Genius* series. In association with his writing, Matt also delivers writing workshops in schools.

Cover illustration by Dan Leydon.
To learn more about Dan, visit danleydon.com
To purchase his artwork visit etsy.com/shop/footynews
Or just follow him on Twitter @danleydon

TABLE OF CONTENTS

ACKNOWLEDGEMENTS

First of all I'd like to thank everyone at Bonnier Books for supporting me and for running the ever-expanding UFH ship so smoothly. Writing stories for the next generation of football fans is both an honour and a pleasure. Thanks also to my agent, Nick Walters, for helping to keep my dream job going, year after year.

Next up, an extra big cheer for all the teachers, booksellers and librarians who have championed these books, and, of course, for the readers. The success of this series is truly down to you.

Okay, onto friends and family. I wouldn't be writing this series if it wasn't for my brother Tom. I owe him so much and I'm very grateful for his belief in me as an author. I'm also very grateful to the rest of my family, especially Mel, Noah, Nico, and of course Mum and Dad. To my parents, I owe my biggest passions: football and books. They're a real inspiration for everything I do.

Pang, Will, Mills, Doug, Naomi, John, Charlie, Sam, Katy, Ben, Karen, Ana (and anyone else I forgot) – thanks for all the love and laughs, but sorry, no I won't be getting 'a real job' anytime soon!

And finally, I couldn't have done any of this without Iona's encouragement and understanding. Much love to you, and of course to Arlo, the ultimate hero of all. I hope we get to enjoy these books together one day.

CHAPTER 1

UP FOR THE (EFL) CUP!

26 February 2023, Wembley Stadium
As the clock ticked towards kick-off, Wembley Stadium was packed and split straight down the middle. To the left of the centre-spot, the red of Manchester United, and to the right, the black-and-white stripes of Newcastle United. What an amazing atmosphere, what an exciting event! It was almost time for the battle to begin...

Toon, Toon, Black and White Army!
Glory, glory Man United!

Many of the Newcastle players were about to make their first appearance at Wembley, and in a cup final of any kind. The Manchester United team, on the other hand, was packed with experienced superstars, as shown by the three men who led the way:

Captain Bruno Fernandes;

Then goalkeeper David de Gea;

And then the club's new midfield hero, Casemiro.

The Spanish League, the Spanish Cup, the UEFA Super Cup, the FIFA Club World Cup, and of course, the UEFA Champions League – the Brazilian had won them all with Real Madrid, and now just six months after joining Manchester United, he was already one of their most important players.

Back in August 2022, when he watched Manchester United lose 4–0 to Brentford, Casemiro could have panicked and pulled out of his big-money move to England. But no – instead, he calmly said to his agent, 'Tell them I'll fix this.'

And game by game, that was exactly what he had done, taking control and charge of the Manchester United midfield. With his calm passing and clever interceptions, Casemiro had helped lead his new team up the Premier League table – to ninth place, then seventh, then all the way up to third – and all the way to Wembley too, for this, the 2023 EFL Cup Final. Now, only Newcastle United stood between them and their first trophy in six long years…

Bring it on! As he walked past the cup and onto the pitch, Casemiro stared straight ahead, fully focused on his task: winning. Yes, he definitely knew how to do that – after all, this was the twentieth final of his football career, and he had won seventeen of them! He was determined to step up for Manchester United when they needed him most, just like he had for Real Madrid, and show what a big-game player he was.

Let's gooooooooooo!

For the first thirty minutes, however, it was a classic, cagey cup final, with very few chances for either team. Then two minutes later, Newcastle passed their way through the Manchester United defence, and Allan Saint-Maximin nearly scored. Uh-oh, it really wasn't looking good for The Reds…

But Casemiro kept calm and carried the ball forward like usual, over the halfway line. With two Newcastle players pressing him, he passed it on to Marcus Rashford, who was fouled as he tried to dribble through. *Free kick!*

A chance for Manchester United, at last! As Luke Shaw placed the ball down, their best headers of the ball made their way into the box: tall striker Wout Weghorst, centre-backs Lisandro Martínez and Raphaël Varane, and Casemiro. His first goal for his new club had been a last-minute looping header against Chelsea; could he grab another one now, in an even more important match?

While the ball curled its way into the middle, Casemiro made a run between three Newcastle defenders and then jumped up and powered his head towards it. *BOOM!* The ball flew low and hard into the bottom corner. *1–0!*

Goooooooooooooooooooooaaaaaaaaaaaaaaaaalllllllllllllll llllllllllll!!!!!!!!!!!!!!!!!

While the Manchester United fans and players went wild, Casemiro just jogged over to the corner flag, looking as cool as ever. Scoring the opening goal in the cup final? No big deal! But really, it was a massive moment, a potentially trophy-winning moment.

'Come onnnnnnnn!' cheered Bruno and Diogo

Dalot, wrapping their arms around him. Soon, he was surrounded by happy, smiling teammates who wanted hugs and high-fives, especially his fellow Brazilians Fred and Antony.

'Bom trabalho, amigo!'

While he walked back towards the halfway line, Casemiro let his own face relax into a smile too, but only a little one. No doubt VAR would be checking for offside, and who knew what the outcome would be? After an anxious wait, however, the goal was given, and this time, Casemiro celebrated with a passionate punch of the air. Advantage Manchester United!

Six minutes later, Casemiro was back in his own half, doing his defensive work. He cleared the ball down the line to Marcus, who flicked it on to Wout, who dribbled forward at the Newcastle defence. On the edge of the box, he slipped a return pass through to Marcus, whose shot deflected off Sven Botman and into the net. *2–0!*

Suddenly, Manchester United looked unstoppable! Job done, final over, trophy won? No, no, no, with all his big-game experience, Casemiro wasn't going to get carried away. They still had plenty more work to do before the 2023 EFL Cup was officially theirs.

Just before half-time, Casemiro was celebrating again, but no, he hadn't scored another goal; he had won a goal-kick for his team! After chasing back and forcing his fellow Brazilian Joelinton to dribble the ball off the pitch, Casemiro roared up at the Manchester United supporters in the crowd, who roared right back. He was a real fans' favourite already, and a teammates' favourite too.

'Yesssssss!' and 'Thanks, mate!' yelled Diogo, Raphaël and Lisandro as they all gave him hugs and high-fives. For defenders, Casemiro was an absolute dream to play with.

In the second half, Manchester United attacked again and again, but they couldn't quite score a third goal. Most importantly, though, they didn't concede any goals at the other end; Casemiro helped make sure of that. With calm authority, he patrolled the middle of the pitch, winning balls and playing simple passes. A late foul on Joelinton eventually earned him a yellow card, but never mind, before long, the final whistle blew. Manchester United had won the 2023 EFL Cup!

Campeones, Campeones, Olé! Olé! Olé!

Glory, glory Man United!

Out on the Wembley pitch, the players bounced up and down together in absolute delight. They were about to lift another trophy, at last! And who was there at the centre of the excited circle? Yes, Casemiro, their first goalscorer and Man of the Match – already, he was at the centre of everything great for Manchester United. What an instant impact he had made on his new team! Another final, another victory, another trophy – the boy from Brazil was just born to win.

CHAPTER 2

DIFFICULT DAYS IN SÃO JOSÉ DOS CAMPOS

On a hot summer's evening in the east of Brazil, a young boy sat in the shade on the cracked doorstep outside a house. For a while, he dug holes in the dirt with a stick, but when that got boring, he swapped to kicking at the stones beneath his bare feet. So, why was he there? Perhaps he was just waiting for time to pass and the temperature to cool down, or perhaps he was waiting for someone, a special someone to arrive. It was difficult to tell at first.

But all of a sudden, there was the sound of footsteps coming down the street towards him. The boy looked up and then jumped up, a beaming smile spreading across his chubby face. It could only mean one thing:

he *had* been waiting for someone, and that special someone had arrived, at last.

'Mamãe!' he shouted, running towards the woman and throwing his arms around her neck.

'Ahh Carlinhos!' the woman replied, showering her son with kisses and love. 'You know, you don't have to wait here for me every day – you should be out having fun with your friends instead!'

But no, Carlos Henrique Casimiro was exactly where he wanted to be each evening: greeting his mum when she finally returned from her tiring job as a housekeeper. As the eldest of the three children, it was his job to help and protect her, as well as his younger siblings, Lucas and Bianca. Their dad had walked out and left the family a few years earlier, and so now Magda was their everything.

Even with their amazing Mamãe there to look after them, however, life was still a real struggle for the Casimiro family. It was like that for a lot of people in São José dos Campos, their city in the east of Brazil, in between São Paulo and Rio de Janeiro. Wages were low and well-paid jobs were hard to find. Thanks to all

Magda's hard work as a housekeeper, each and every
day of the week, she was just about able to provide
enough food and clothes for her children, but sadly they
couldn't afford a nice, fixed home of their own. Instead,
they mostly lived at Magda's sister's house, all four of
them trying to sleep in one small, cramped room.

And what about all the little things that most kids
want, like toys, sweets and tasty treats? No, there was
never enough money for those. Mamãe's answer was
always the same: 'I'll buy it for you next time.' That
'next time' never came, though, and so eventually,
Carlos just stopped asking for anything.

Life was hard, but at least he had his Mamãe by
his side. Her love and support were enough for now.
One day, when he was older, he would get a good
job and look after her, just like she looked after him.
Hopefully, he would even earn enough money to
buy her the house of her own that she so deserved.
That was the dream, and young Carlos was already
working towards it. Yes, by the age of six, he had
already found his way: football.

'Hey, you're getting *REALLY* good at this!' Monica

said to her cousin Carlos one day as they kicked a ball around together in the dusty streets of São José dos Campos. 'You know what, you should come and play for my team – want me to ask my coach for you?'

Carlos didn't need to think about it; he nodded his head straight away, with a wide smile and eager eyes. Of course, he wanted to play for a proper team! Wasn't that what every kid wanted, especially in a football-crazy country like Brazil? Carlos had been practising his skills for ages, waiting for a chance like this.

'Okay, cool, I'll ask him at training tonight,' his cousin promised.

Monica's team was called Moreira and her coach was Nilton de Jesus Moreira himself, the man who had started the club a year earlier. His mission was to keep the local kids happy, healthy and out of trouble through the power of football. As Monica told him all about her gifted young cousin, Moreira listened carefully and then asked an important question:

'Can he play in goal?'

Monica was the first-choice goalkeeper for the Moreira girls' team, but they needed a back-up, especially for training exercises. Maybe this boy could start off there. He was still only six years old, after all.

She shrugged and smiled. 'Sure – he'll be happy to play any position!'

'Okay, well why not?!' Moreira said. 'Tell your cousin he can come down and join in next week.'

'Thanks, Coach – see you then!'

Carlos was delighted when he heard the good news, and he gave his cousin a big hug to say thanks. Hurray – his famous football career was about to begin! When the day arrived and he walked into the Moreira training ground for the first time with Monica, he felt no fear or nerves. Instead, he was buzzing with excitement and confidence. He couldn't wait! This was it; his chance to show off his skills to the world, starting with the Moreira coach.

'Welcome to the club – Monica has told me lots about you!' the coach greeted the boy warmly. 'So today, you'll be starting off as a goalkeeper with the girls' team, and we'll see how it goes. Okay?'

'Ok, thanks, *senhor*,' Carlos replied politely, but Moreira noticed a real determination in the six-year-old's face. And look at that puffed-out chest – the kid was bursting with self-belief!

Surprise, surprise – Carlos didn't stay as a back-up keeper for long. No, once the coach saw his talent out on the pitch, with the ball at his feet, he soon moved him up to the boys' Under-9s team, where he quickly stood out as one of the star players.

'Wow, this kid is special!' Moreira thought to himself. It wasn't that Carlos was taller, bigger or stronger than the others; it was that he was more powerful in the way that he moved across the pitch, both in and out of possession. He loved to control the game with calm touches and clever passes, but he also loved the battle to win the ball back. He just wanted to be at the centre of everything.

'Well done, Carlos – great tackle!'

'That's it – look up and pass to a teammate in space!'

Moreira was very impressed, and as he watched, his mind raced with questions and ideas. How were they going to make the most of this gifted young footballer? What could they do to help him improve? And perhaps most importantly, what was the boy's best position? In his first tournament, Carlos played as a striker and scored lots of goals. He was like a little Romário, the Number 11 for the Brazil national team.

But when he played as a winger, Carlos was like a little Rivaldo, and when he played as a full-back, he was like a little Roberto Carlos. The boy could do it all and shine anywhere on the pitch, but Moreira liked him best at the heart of the midfield, like Dunga or Mauro Silva. There, he could make full use of his power, his quick feet, and his calm, clever football brain. While it wasn't a position that came with lots of goals or glory, it was one of the most important on the pitch.

'Midfield is where everything happens,' Moreira explained to his young superstar, 'and you get to be at the centre of it all.'

Carlos loved the sound of that, and he loved playing football – every single second of it. It was fun, he clearly had a gift for the game, and it was also a way for him to escape from the struggles in his home life. At his aunt's house, it was so cramped and chaotic that he often asked his teammates if he could stay with them to get a better night's sleep before a match.

One day, Carlos told himself, everything would be better and easier, but to get there, he had a long, hard road ahead of him...

From the Under-9s, he moved up to the Under-11s, and as he got older, Moreira became much more than just a football coach for him. He was a father-figure too, someone who helped Carlos in lots of different ways: paying his match fees, finding him new football boots, even organising his first passport.

With Magda working so hard every day to provide for the family, she sadly couldn't go and watch her son play. Instead, she had to trust Moreira to look after Carlos at the football club and keep him away from the darker sides of life in São José dos Campos.

So far, that plan was working perfectly, and just in case Carlos needed any extra motivation to follow his football dream, the 2002 FIFA World Cup was about to begin.

CHAPTER 3

WORLD CUP FEVER

'Carlinhos, are you excited about the World Cup?'
Magda asked her son one evening as they stood
together in the kitchen, preparing dinner.

At last, the topic that he really wanted to talk about!
'Yes, Mamãe, I can't wait,' Carlos replied eagerly.
'Brazil are going to win it again and I'm going to
watch every game!'

Magda smiled and rolled her eyes – what was it
about Brazilians and football? Every four years, the
country caught World Cup fever and it spread like
wildfire, from the shops and bars, to the streets and
houses. Suddenly, every wall was splashed with the
colours of the national flag – yellow and green – and

decorated with paintings of the country's football heroes. Until the tournament was over, it was all anyone cared about, and it always ended in tears: sometimes of joy, but usually of sorrow…

'So, what time will the matches start?' Magda asked, knowing full well that she probably wouldn't be able to watch a single minute, even if she wanted to.

'Half-past three, six and half-past eight!' Carlos said, hoping that would be enough to satisfy his mum's curiosity.

'In the afternoon and early evening?' She shrugged as she chopped up the vegetables. 'Okay, that's not so bad. At least, you won't be staying up late at night—'

'No, Mamãe – in the morning.'

Suddenly, Magda stopped chopping. 'What, so some of the games start at 3.30am? Why?!'

'They're playing in Japan and South Korea,' Carlos explained. 'Please Mamãe, I have to watch it all – IT'S THE WORLD CUP!'

Magda ignored her son's pleading, puppy dog eyes and took a moment to think. 'Hmmm, well it is the summer holidays, I suppose. So, if you can wake yourself up in time, then you can go and watch the games.'

'Thanks, Mamãe – you're the best!' Carlos cried, giving her a massive hug.

As a ten-year-old, this was his first time at catching World Cup fever, and the first time was always the strongest. Over the next few weeks, Carlos didn't miss a single minute of any match that Brazil played:

The tense 2–1 win over Turkey, thanks to a late Rivaldo penalty;

The 4–0 thrashing of China, where Roberto Carlos scored a stunning free kick;

The 5–2 thriller against Costa Rica…

Yes, the 3am wake-up was totally worth it for that last one – what a game and what a dream team! Brazil were just so exciting to watch with all of their amazing attackers:

The flying wing-backs Cafu and Roberto Carlos;

The little midfield playmaker Juninho Paulista;

And then 'The 3 Rs': Rivaldo, Ronaldinho, and Carlos's favourite player of all, Ronaldo. Four years earlier, he had fallen ill before the World Cup final and

Brazil had lost to France, but now 'O Fenômeno' was back, looking better than ever. He had scored three goals in three games already!

With so many superstars in the Brazil team, the big question was: how was anyone going to beat them?

Belgium did their best in the Round of 16, but in the second half, Rivaldo was just too brilliant for them.

'Brasil, Brasil!' Carlos cheered.

England took the lead in the quarter-finals, but Ronaldinho turned the game around.

'Brasil, Brasil!'

In the semi-finals, Turkey held strong for the first half, but early in the second, Ronaldo tore through their defence with speed and skill to score the winner.

'Brasil, Brasil!'

After 1994 and 1998, now in 2002 they were through to their third World Cup final in a row, and Carlos couldn't wait. Their opponents, Germany, were a very good team but surely they were no match for Brazil? As the tournament went on, their team was getting stronger and stronger. They still had the flying wing-backs and the '3 Rs' in attack, but they also now looked more solid in defence too. Their three centre-backs were all playing well, and they had found the perfect balance in midfield, with Gilberto Silva sitting deep and Kléberson running box to box all game long. Much better!

'Moreira was right,' Carlos thought to himself. 'Central midfield really is one of the most important positions on the pitch!'

When the World Cup final kicked off in Yokohama, Japan, Carlos was feeling very confident, and so were most of the other 180 million people watching back home in Brazil. Yes, that trophy was going to be theirs yet again, but only if they could win the game!

Ronaldinho slipped a great pass through to Ronaldo... but with a poke of his left boot, he sent a shot spinning wide.

Oooooooohhhhhhhhhhhhhh!

Kléberson dragged his first shot wide, but his second was much better, curling up, up towards the top corner... no, it crashed off the crossbar!

Oooooooohhhhhhhhhhhhhh!

Somehow, at half-time, the score was still 0–0. Oh

dear – was it just not going to be Brazil's day? Staring at the TV screen in São José dos Campos, Carlos never stopped believing. Even when Oliver Neuville hit the post for Germany, he stayed fully positive. As long as Brazil kept playing well, eventually their winning goal would come...

In the sixty-seventh minute, Rivaldo got the ball just outside the penalty area, shifted it out of his feet, and *BANG!* blasted it straight at Oliver Kahn. It should have been a pretty simple save for such an excellent keeper, but somehow, the ball squirmed out of his gloves, and straight to... Ronaldo!

Goooooooooooooooooooooaaaaaaaaaaaaaaaalllllllllllllll lllllllllllll!!!!!!!!!!!!!!!!!!!!

'Yessssssssssssssssssssssssssssssss!' yelled the thousands of Brazil supporters in the stadium in Japan, as well as Carlos and all the other 180 million people celebrating back home. At last, they were winning in the World Cup final!

Now, could they hold on for victory? In fact, Brazil did better than just hold on. Twelve minutes later, Rivaldo dummied Kléberson's pass from the right, and the ball ran through to Ronaldo, who calmly curled a shot into the bottom corner. *2–0!*

Game over, World Cup won! There were still ten minutes to go, but Carlos and his fellow Brazilians were already getting the party started.

Brasil, Brasil!

CAMPEÕES! CAMPEÕES!

What a night, and what a night to be Brazilian! That proud feeling was something that young Carlos would never, ever forget, and it inspired him to dream even bigger than before. Why not? One day, he wanted to be out there wearing the famous yellow shirt, and winning a World Cup for his country. How incredible would that be?

CHAPTER 4

SETTING OFF FOR SÃO PAULO

While that World Cup dream was still a long way off, Carlos's football career was definitely moving in the right direction. Moreira were no longer just a small local club; they were a team on the rise, taking on tougher opponents every season. In 2003, they played a match against Santos, one of the best and biggest clubs in Brazil.

Pelé, 'The King of Football', had played for Santos, but was Carlos nervous about facing such a famous team? No, not at all! Just like on his first day at Moreira, he was buzzing with excitement and confidence. He couldn't wait! This was it; his chance to show off his skills against Santos and test himself against their new 'next big thing', a silky-skilled kid called Neymar Jr.

'Come on, we can do this!' Carlos told his teammates before kick-off with real belief in his voice. Sadly, they didn't end up winning the match, but he did a very impressive job in midfield, and showed he could certainly compete with any superstar from Santos. Soon, Carlos and Neymar Jr would be facing each other a lot more frequently...

As his small team became more and more successful, Nilton Moreira had formed an agreement with their biggest local club, São Paulo. Careca, Cafu, Kaká – so many of Brazil's best players had played for them over the years. But while São Paulo were a huge club with lots of history, they were also always on the lookout for stars of the future. Finding 'The Next Ronaldo' before anyone else wasn't easy, especially in an enormous, football-crazy country like Brazil. That's why they wanted agreements with smaller teams in nearby cities, like Moreira in São José dos Campos. The deal was simple: São Paulo would send scouts to watch Moreira's top young talents, and if they liked what they saw, they would invite players to go for trials at the academy.

'Looking forward to doing football business with you!' Moreira said with a smile as he shook hands with the São Paulo scouts. 'First up, I've got this kid in the Under-11s who can play all over the pitch, but I think defensive midfield is where he'll shine the brightest...'

By the time he played that match against Neymar Jr's Santos, Carlos was already being watched by the São Paulo scouts. But it was only a few years later, aged thirteen, when he finally made the massive move to the club's academy in Cotia.

See you later, Moreira – Carlos was setting off for São Paulo! As he waved goodbye to São José dos Campos, however, he felt a real mix of emotions. Of course, he was delighted and proud to be joining one of the best clubs in Brazil, but he couldn't help feeling a little scared and uncertain too. This was his first time away from home – how would he cope in a big new city, without his siblings and his beloved Mamãe there by his side?

'Don't worry, you'll be able to come back and visit us,' his mum had reassured him, but when and how often? Every weekend? Once a month? Once a year?

Luckily, when he arrived in Cotia, Carlos found plenty to distract him. Woah, after his difficult early days in São José dos Campos, it was like entering a completely different world! At the São Paulo academy, not only could he eat as much food as he wanted, but he also had his own room, a TV to watch, and even air conditioning.

'This is the LIFE!' Carlos thought to himself as he relaxed on his bed after a tiring training session, but he never forgot about his family struggling back home. Because although this was his own football dream that he was following, he was also doing it for them. If he became a successful, professional player, he would earn enough money to look after everyone: Lucas, Bianca, Mamãe, Moreira, plus his aunt and cousins as well.

That was Carlos's big plan, but just as he was settling into his new life in São Paulo, he suffered a major setback. At first, he thought his body was just really tired because of all the extra effort he was putting into training, but then he also started to feel sick and feverish.

'Tell Coach that I can't train today,' he told his teammates from his bed. What was wrong with him? He didn't feel like eating anything or doing anything, except lying there sleeping. That wasn't like him at all...

It turned out that Carlos had a disease called hepatitis, the São Paulo doctors discovered. Hepatitis?! That sounded really serious, but the doctors had good news and bad news for him.

The good news? With enough rest, Carlos would be able to recover and get back to playing football again.

Phew, what a relief!

And the bad news? 'Enough rest' didn't mean a few days or weeks – it meant months.

'Nooooo, really?' Carlos groaned in his hospital bed. The thought of months without football was unbearable. What would he do instead? How would he fill all those long hours? And the timing was terrible – he would have so much catching up to do at the São Paulo academy!

'Yes, really – you've lost a lot of weight, Carlos,' the doctors explained, 'and your body is still very weak. We need to build your strength back up first.'

Fiiiiiine! During the next few months, there were many frustrating, restless days when Carlos felt like he had failed and should just give up on his football dream and go home, but fortunately he didn't. With the support of Moreira, his Mamãe, and his coaches at São Paulo, he kept going and battled his way back to full fitness. Whenever he felt low, he thought about his family back home and the plan he was working towards.

'Come on – I can do this,' Carlos told himself, as his determination came rushing back.

At last, after three months away from football, he was finally ready to return to the pitch. Hurray! Now, it was time for Carlos to show the São Paulo coaches what an incredible player he could be.

CHAPTER 5

A TRIP TO OLD TRAFFORD

The football at São Paulo was a big step-up for Carlos, with tougher training sessions and even more talented teammates. There was a creative playmaker called Oscar who could dribble and pass like Kaká, a speedy, skilful winger called Lucas Moura who could dazzle his way past any defender, and a forward called Lucas Piazon who couldn't stop scoring.

Could Carlos really compete with these wonderkids? Oh yes, he had the talent and the determination to rise to every challenge. After his months away, he was more motivated than ever, and the better players around him helped to bring out the best in him. Before long, he was one of the most important players in Bruno Petri's youth team, as well as the captain.

'That's it, Carlão – quick, clever passes!'

'What a performance today, Warrior!'

Carlos was exactly the kind of character that coaches loved to work with: calm, dedicated, and always eager to listen and learn. And out on the pitch, he was blessed with a special combination of power and skill. He was so big and strong that sometimes he looked like a man playing amongst boys, but then on the ball, he also had that classic Brazilian flair. His touch was excellent, he could pass well with both feet, he could dribble past opponents, and he could score goals too. There was nothing Carlos couldn't do, and no position that he couldn't play, but Petri agreed with Moreira: defensive midfield was where he shone the brightest.

'As a "Number Six", you can control the game and become a football superstar,' Petri told his young captain.

'Thanks, Senhor!' Carlos replied happily. That was the plan that he was working towards, day by day. He knew that there was still a long way to go, and lots of challenges ahead, but he was ready to rise to every single one.

In 2007, aged fifteen, Carlos was part of the São Paulo youth team that travelled to England to compete in the Nike Cup, one of the top youth tournaments in the world. Some 90,000 clubs had entered the competition from forty different countries, and yet São Paulo had successfully managed to qualify for the finals in Manchester. They had already been crowned South American Champions, but could they now go all the way and become World Champions?

'Yeah, we can beat anyone!' Carlos announced, feeling as confident as ever.

The aeroplane, the hotel, the cold, wet English weather – wow, what an experience! The whole trip was a whirlwind for Carlos, but on the football pitch, he managed to stay focused on doing what he did best: winning. With his calm and quality in midfield, São Paulo made it through to the semi-finals, where they beat Schalke 04 from Germany. Hurray, they were into the Nike Cup Final!

'Well done, boys – what a win!' Petri cheered proudly at the final whistle. 'Right, this calls for a special reward – who wants to go and get some pizza?'

'Meeeeeeeeeeeeeeeeeeeeeeeee!'

As they sat there eating their well-earned pizzas, the São Paulo players were all buzzing with excitement. In the final, they would face the Spanish giants Barcelona, and that wasn't even the best bit. The big game would be played at... Old Trafford. Yes, 'The Theatre of Dreams', the famous home of Manchester United!

'Woah!' Carlos thought to himself, and that 'Woah!' got even louder when they walked into the stadium and started looking around. He had seen big stadiums before, like São Paulo's Morumbi, but there was something special about Old Trafford. So many amazing moments in football history had taken place here, and so many amazing players had called it home: David Beckham, Ryan Giggs, Paul Scholes, Rio Ferdinand, Wayne Rooney, Cristiano Ronaldo... The list went on and on and on.

As he stood there, mouth open in awe, Carlos dared to dream about what it would be like to be a

Manchester United player one day, walking out in front of adoring 75,000 fans. Wouldn't that be wonderful?

Now wasn't the time for fantasy, though. São Paulo still had one more match to win, and Carlos was determined to beat Barcelona to the trophy.

'Let's goooooooooooooooo, guys!'

Unfortunately, with Scholes there watching in the crowd, São Paulo had to settle for second place in the Nike Cup. After a strong start, they faded away, and early in the second half, Barcelona grabbed what turned out to be the winning goal.

Noooooooooooooooooooooooo! At the final whistle, Carlos collapsed to the grass, his eyes filling with tears. All that hard work and they had lost 1–0 – what a horrible feeling it was to get so close to glory!

By the time the São Paulo team travelled back to Brazil a day later, most of the players were feeling more positive about the experience. Never mind, they had done really well to reach the final, hadn't they? Carlos, however, was still furious on the flight home. He refused to talk to anyone, even his manager.

'Come on, cheer up, Carlão! What's wrong?' Petri

asked eventually.

His captain gave him a fierce look, and replied, 'I don't think we should have had pizza before the final. We should have waited until after we won the trophy.'

Petri just nodded and walked away, but in his head, he was thinking, 'Wow, that kid cares so much about winning!'

It was already clear that Carlos had the right mentality to become a very successful footballer, and the talent too. Maybe he might even get to play at Old Trafford again one day, for the mighty Manchester United? Who knew – if he kept progressing at his current speed, anything was possible!

In the meantime, Carlos was soon setting off on more international adventures, this time to Chile and Nigeria...

CHAPTER 6

BRAZIL'S BRIGHT YOUNG THINGS

In early 2009, Brazil Under-17s coach Luiz Antônio Nizzo announced his twenty-player squad for the upcoming South American Championships in Chile. So, which of the country's many young superstars would make the important list? It read:

...05 Elivélton (Santos),

06 Dodô (Corinthians),

07 Dudu (Cruzeiro),

08 João Pedro (Atlético Mineiro),

09 Willen (Vasco da Gama),

10 Philippe Coutinho (Vasco da Gama)...

And way down at the very bottom...

20 Carlos Henrique Venancio Casimiro (São Paulo).

Hurray, Carlos was in! What an honour, what a dream come true – he was about to become a Brazil international! He couldn't wait to represent his country in the tournament, and follow in the footsteps of his football heroes like Ronaldo and Ronaldinho. Plus, if Brazil won it, or finished in the top four, they would also qualify for the U-17 World Cup in Nigeria.

'Let's do this!' Carlos told his new teammate, Philippe. Together, they led their country to a 4–0 win over Paraguay, and then a 3–0 win over Peru. *Olé! Olé!* – the samba boys were flying! Despite a surprise 2–0 defeat to Colombia, Brazil still finished top of Group A. They were through to the tournament final, where they would play the winners of Group B... Argentina! Yes, South America's two top national teams were going head-to-head yet again.

'We *have* to win this,' Carlos told his teammates before kick-off with that determined look on his face. It wasn't just a football match; it was a battle for national pride.

When Philippe scored early in the second half to give Brazil a 2–0 lead, it looked like game over and battle won, but no, Argentina came fighting back to take the final all the way to... PENALTIES!

Although Carlos wasn't selected as one of Brazil's first five takers, he was always ready to step up if needed. And he was; after five spot-kicks each, the two teams were tied at 2–2, so the shoot-out went to sudden death. Ooooooooh, it was so tense now! Who would be the first poor player to miss?

Not Carlos! He was ice-cold under pressure. He calmly walked forward to take Brazil's seventh penalty and made no mistake from the spot. *BANG!... GOAL!* Then after a quick punch of the air and a 'Come on!' for his keeper, he made his way back to the halfway line. Job done.

A few spot-kicks later, it was all over, and the winners were... Brazil!

'Yesssssssssssssssss!' Carlos cried out as he sprinted over to celebrate with all his teammates. They had achieved their goal; they were the Champions of South America!

And they had done it even without their most highly rated young superstar: Santos's next big thing,

Neymar Jr. He would be back in time for the U-17
World Cup in October, and with him added to
their already-exciting attack, Brazil would surely be
unbeatable! No wonder they were now the favourites
to win the whole competition.

In tournament football, however, anything can
happen, and in Nigeria, Brazil's bright young things
really struggled to shine. Did they arrive at the
World Cup feeling over-confident? Maybe a bit, but
they also came up against three very strong, well-
organised teams.

For their opening game against Japan, Nizzo moved
Neymar Jr straight into the starting line-up, which
meant someone else would have to drop down to the
subs bench. Elivélton? João Pedro? No, they would
play together in central midfield. Instead, it was Carlos
who missed out.

Although he was disappointed, he didn't complain.
It was only the first match, and hopefully he'd be able
to work his way into the team as the tournament went
on. But as Carlos watched and supported his country
from the sidelines, he suddenly began to worry about

Brazil's chances.

1–0... 1–1,

2–1... 2–2...

Twice, they took the lead, and twice, they let Japan equalise. Some of the attacking play between Philippe and Neymar Jr was sublime, but where was the tough tackling, the solid defending, the control in midfield? In the end, it took a last-minute free kick to win the game 3–2.

Phew! Brazil were off to a shaky start, but surely things would soon get better?

No – in their next match against Mexico, they had lots of possession but let in a sloppy goal and lost 1–0. What was going on? All that attacking talent in the team, and they couldn't even score!

'This tournament is turning into a disaster!' Carlos moaned to himself, sitting miserably on the bench.

Brazil now had to win their final group game against Switzerland to stay in the World Cup. With the pressure on, the manager moved Carlos into central midfield alongside Elivélton and João Pedro to try to keep things calm and steady.

That was the plan, anyway, but in the twenty-first minute, Switzerland took a surprise lead. After a great save from Brazil's goalkeeper Alisson, striker Nassim Ben Khalifa was there in the right place to head in the rebound. *1–0!* As he watched the ball cross the goal-line, Carlos's heart sank. Uh-oh – Brazil's task had just got a whole lot harder.

For the rest of the match, they attacked and attacked, but just like against Mexico, they couldn't get the goals they needed. Sadly for them, the Swiss keeper was on fire, making save after save after save. And even when one of their shots did get past him, there was always a defender on the line to clear the ball away.

'Argggh, it's no use – we're about to get knocked out!' Carlos muttered angrily as he was subbed off after sixty minutes.

He was right; when the final whistle blew, the Brazil players fell to the floor in despair and disbelief. With three games, three goals, one win and two defeats, their World Cup was over already. Noooooooooo! How? Why? What an embarrassing exit for the tournament favourites! They were so much better than that.

It was another furious flight home for Carlos, but by the time he arrived back in Brazil, he felt determined to turn things around and make up for the nightmare in Nigeria. He just had to hope that he would get another chance to shine brightly for his country.

CHAPTER 7

HERE COMES... CASEMIRO!

One disappointing tournament wasn't going to get Carlos down. Back at São Paulo, he continued his incredible rise to the top. In January 2010, he helped the Under-20s to win the São Paulo Youth Cup, beating Neymar Jr's Santos on penalties in the final.

Campeões, Campeões, Olé! Olé! Olé!

Carlos was delighted to win one of the biggest junior competitions in Brazil, but he soon had his sights set even higher: the São Paulo first team. Why not? Attacking midfielder Oscar had already made the jump during the 2009 season, playing thirteen matches, and he was only six months older. Surely there was space for a new Number Six too?

'I'm ready for this!' Carlos told himself and anyone else who would listen.

He spent pre-season training with the first team, and for São Paulo's second league game against Esporte Clube Vitória, he was named on the subs bench. Even though Carlos didn't come on, it was still a great experience and it was still progress. He could feel his debut getting closer and closer.

A week later, on 25 July, his big day arrived. When the São Paulo manager Ricardo Gomes announced the team, there was Carlos's name, and not on the subs bench, but in the actual starting line-up!

'Yesssssssss!' he wanted to scream with excitement, but instead, he sat there quietly, heart pounding, and tried to focus on the football match ahead. And who were São Paulo playing that day? Yes, you guessed it – Neymar Jr's Santos!

'I feel like we play against each other every week!' Carlos joked as they hugged before kick-off. Thanks to their trips away with the Brazil national team, they were now good friends, but not for the next ninety minutes. No, until the final whistle blew, they were rivals.

Wearing the number '29' on the back of his black and red-striped shirt, Carlos was determined to make a strong first impression in front of the São Paulo fans. But he didn't just race forward on the attack at every opportunity because that wasn't his job. No, his job was to stay back, protect the defence, and control the game from deep. So, he used his power to fight hard for every ball, and kept his passing quick and accurate.

'That's it – well played, Carlão!'

Although Santos won the match 1–0, Carlos walked off the pitch feeling proud of his own performance and hoping that it would be the first of many.

It was; from that game forward, Carlos became a regular in the São Paulo starting line-up. And the more he played, the more he showed what an all-round midfielder he was. As well as doing the dirty work in defence, the kid also had a lot of attacking strengths:

• **Heading**

In a crowded penalty area against Cruzeiro, Carlos used his height to jump up and flick Jean's free kick down into the bottom corner. *1–0!*

*Goooooooooooooooooooaaaaaaaaaaaaaaaalllllllllllll
llllllllllll!!!!!!!!!!!!!!!!!!!*

Hurray, his first for São Paulo! As Carlos jogged
over to the supporters, pointing proudly at the badge
on his shirt, Fernandão gave him a big hug, lifting
him off his feet.

'Yessss, you hero!' the forward cheered.

- **Shooting**

It would be a while before Carlos scored his first
long-range rocket, but against Atlético Mineiro, he
showed that he still had his old striker's instincts in
the six-yard box. As the ball dropped towards him, he
watched it carefully onto the side of his right foot and
calmly volleyed it in. *1–0!*

*Goooooooooooooooooooaaaaaaaaaaaaaaaalllllllllllll
llllllllllll!!!!!!!!!!!!!!!!!!!*

Wow, Carlos was really flying in the first team now!
He fell to his knees in front of the fans, and all his
teammates rushed over to congratulate him. The last
and longest hug came from Lucas Moura, his friend
since their early days at the academy. How wonderful
it was to be living their dreams together!

• Passing

Once he felt settled into the São Paulo team, Carlos began to push forward more often and play more creative passes. Instead of sideways or backwards, he looked forwards for teammates on the run. Against Guarani, he slid a perfect, first-time pass through to Marlos, who fired a shot past the keeper. *1–0!*

'Thanks, mate!' Marlos shouted, throwing his arms around Carlos.

Suddenly, the wider football world was starting to talk about São Paulo's young midfield maestro, although they weren't calling him 'Carlos' or 'Carlão' or 'Carlinhos', or even his proper surname, 'Casimiro'. No, weirdly, he was now known as Casemiro.

It had all begun with a simple printing mistake. During one of his early matches for São Paulo, the club got his name wrong and wrote 'Casemiro', with an 'e' rather than an 'i'. He was planning to tell them after the game, but he played really well in that match, and so superstitious Carlos changed his mind and decided to stick with Casemiro. Why not? It was close enough!

Unfortunately, Casemiro's first senior season faded

away to a slightly disappointing end, but his second was a different story.

By 2011, São Paulo's young stars weren't just prospects for the future anymore; they were key players for the present, and they had the shirt numbers to prove it: '7' for Lucas and '8' for Casemiro.

'Right, let's do this!' they cheered excitedly.

The club's new Number 10, Brazilian legend Rivaldo, was supposed to be the team's main superstar, but it didn't turn out that way.

In São Paulo's first game of the season against Fluminense, Casemiro set up the first goal for Dagoberto, and Lucas scored the second. Lucas grabbed the winner a week later against Figueirense, and then it was Casemiro's turn against Atlético Mineiro. Midway through the first half, his midfield partner Wellington slid the ball across to him just outside the box. What a chance! Casemiro took a touch to control it and then curled an unstoppable shot into the side of the net. *1–0!*

Goooooooooooooooooooooaaaaaaaaaaaaaaaaalllllllllllllll llllllllll!!!!!!!!!!!!!!!!!!!!!

Casemiro was feeling so happy and confident that he even did a little dance over by the corner flag! He was officially in the best form of his football life, and he didn't stop there:

Another goal against Grêmio!

Followed by another assist against Ceará, to set up another goal for Lucas!

'This is so much fun!' they shouted as they celebrated together.

But just when São Paulo's young stars were taking the Brazilian league by storm, the national Under-20 team came calling. Yes, Casemiro was off to play in another World Cup for his country. So, would he be second time lucky?

CHAPTER 8

WORLD CUP DREAM COME TRUE

'Come on, we *have* to do better than we did last time!'
Casemiro told Philippe as they travelled to Colombia
for the Under-20 World Cup. Despite all the success
he'd had at São Paulo in the two years since, the
memories of Nigeria still haunted him. It was time to
put things right and make the Brazilian people proud.

So far, the signs looked positive. They had won the
South American Youth Championships again with
ease, and although they had lost Neymar Jr to the
seniors, the overall squad looked even stronger now.
Casemiro's club teammates Lucas, Oscar and Willian
José were all in, and so were three excellent new
defenders: Danilo, Alex Sandro and Juan Jesus.

But perhaps most importantly of all for Brazil, Casemiro was now their main man in midfield. Alongside Fernando, he was the reliable rock at the centre of the team.

Despite all that, however, when the World Cup began, Brazil got off to another shaky start. A 1–1 draw really wasn't the result they were hoping for against Egypt, and their only goal came from Danilo in defence.

Casemiro wasn't panicking this time, though. Brazil just needed to find their samba rhythm, that was all. The first thirty minutes against Austria weren't great either, but after that, everything started to click and the goals began to flow…

Henrique finished off a fantastic team move. *1–0!*

Danilo was fouled by the keeper and Philippe scored from the penalty spot. *2–0!*

And Brazil saved the best goal until last. Oscar played the ball forward to Philippe, who flicked it through to Casemiro, who split the Austrian defence with a wonderful pass to Willian José. *3–0!*

'That's more like it!' Their coach, Ney Franco,

clapped and cheered on the sidelines.

Suddenly, Brazil were looking brilliant, and three days later, Philippe grabbed two more goals as they thrashed poor Panama 4–0. Hurray, they were through to the knockout rounds! That was only the first part of the plan completed, though. Carlos and his teammates wanted to go all the way and lift the World Cup trophy.

Brazil cruised past Saudi Arabia in the Round of 16, but beating Spain in the quarter-finals was a much tougher challenge. They had a very talented team featuring Rodrigo, Isco, and Koke, and they dominated the early part of the game, forcing Franco to tweak his tactics a little.

'Casemiro!' he called from the touchline. 'I want you to drop deeper and play as a third centre-back. Then Danilo and Gabriel Silva can push further forward up the wings.'

'Si, Senhor!'

Switching to a new position in the middle of the match? No problem, Casemiro slotted in perfectly, allowing Brazil to get back into the game. Twice, they took the lead but twice, Spain fought back to equalise, until eventually there was only one way to decide the winner: penalties!

'I'll go first,' Casemiro said straight away, no doubt or fear in his mind. He was a leader, and this was the time to show it. So, forward he walked from the halfway line, and once the referee blew his whistle, he calmly fired a shot past the keeper. No problem!

Yesssssssssssssssss!

Boosted by Casemiro's confidence, Danilo and Henrique went next and did the same: three out of three! Soon, Dudu had the chance to win it for Brazil. He stepped up and... scored!

'YESSSSSSSSSSSSS!' the whole team cheered, racing over to celebrate with Dudu and their heroic keeper, Gabriel.

Casemiro wasn't getting carried away just yet, though. Winning two more matches; that's what Brazil needed to focus on. In his mind, he was already moving on to their next game, the World Cup semi-final against... Mexico.

Playing against a very strong, determined defence, Brazil had to show real patience. The second-half minutes ticked by and still they hadn't scored – it was like the Under-17 World Cup all over again! Were Mexico going to score another surprise winning goal?

No, this time, Brazil held their nerve and Henrique stepped up to be their hero. In the eightieth minute, he headed in the first, and then moments later, he scored again. With the last of his energy, Casemiro burst forward from midfield and slipped a perfectly weighted pass through to Dudu on the right, who played the ball across to Henrique. *2–0!*

Job done – Brazil were through to the World Cup final! But when the final whistle blew, Casemiro didn't jump for joy. No, he bent down, took a deep breath of relief, and then walked around the pitch shaking hands with his opponents, like it was any other game.

Getting to a final was great, but the hardest part was still to come: winning it. Casemiro had learned that painful lesson at the Nike Cup years earlier.

In the World Cup final, Brazil faced Portugal, the team that had already knocked out two of the tournament favourites, Argentina and France. They didn't score many goals, but they didn't concede many either – in fact, they hadn't conceded a single goal in their six games so far.

'Let's ruin that record!' Brazil's attackers all agreed, and it only took them five minutes to do that. Oscar's long, swerving free kick flicked off the head of a Portugal defender and flew past the keeper. *1–0!*

What a start in the World Cup final! Portugal, however, didn't panic. Four minutes later, they were level, and in the second half, they scored again to take the lead.

Noooooooooooooooooo!

With the score at 2–1 to Portugal, now it was Brazil's turn to fight back.

'Stay calm!' Casemiro urged his teammates. 'We've still got plenty of time!'

At last, with ten minutes to go, they got their equaliser. Dudu's shot was saved and the rebound fell to Oscar. 2–2!

Phew, game on! Their thrilling World Cup final was heading for extra-time. Now, could either team come up with a winning goal before it went all the way to penalties? From wide on the right wing, Oscar looked up and whipped a high, looping ball into the box. Was it a cross, was it a shot? Who cares because it flew over the Portugal keeper's upstretched arms and landed in the net!

Now it was 3–2 – wow, Brazil were winning again!

This time, Casemiro helped keep everyone composed and they held on for the victory.

And this time, when the final whistle blew, all of their players jumped for joy, including Casemiro. It was time to relax and enjoy the magical moment. He had successfully turned things around and made his dream come true – Brazil were the new World Champions!

CHAPTER 9

PROBLEMS AT SÃO PAULO

Casemiro returned home to Brazil with an Under-20 World Cup winner's medal around his neck and lots of exciting European clubs wanting to sign him:

Tottenham,

Roma,

And even the two big Milan teams, AC and Inter.

Wow, was Casemiro really about to follow in the footsteps of his childhood heroes like Ronaldo and Ronaldinho? It would be another dream come true! He loved the idea of a move to Italy, especially as his good friend and Brazil teammate Philippe was already there, starring for Inter.

'I feel ready to play in Serie A,' Casemiro declared

with confidence.

But for now, he was still at São Paulo, and they were halfway through the Brazilian league season. So far, they were sitting third in the table, just behind Flamengo and Corinthians, but now that they had their bright young stars back from the World Cup, could they push on and win the title?

It was like they'd never been away! Casemiro slotted straight back in alongside Wellington in midfield, Lucas linked up with Dagoberto in attack, and São Paulo were back to their best. Lucas scored a stunning solo goal against Santos, and then Casemiro set up the winner against Figueirense with a fantastic pass through to Rivaldo.

'Welcome back,' the Brazilian legend said with a big smile. 'We've missed you!'

In their next home game against Atlético Mineiro, São Paulo's young superstars linked up in the very first minute. Casemiro raced forward to make a strong, block tackle and the ball ran through to Lucas, who slid a shot past the keeper. *1–0!*

'Come onnnnnn!' they cheered, celebrating

together in front of the fans.

With another win, São Paulo moved up to second place, just two points behind Corinthians. The title race was on!

And for Casemiro, there was more good news to come. In September 2011, he was called up to the Brazil senior squad for the first time and made his debut as a late sub against their big rivals, Argentina. What a moment!

Running on to the field to replace Paulinho, Casemiro didn't feel any nerves or pressure; no, he was just enjoying his football. A few days later, back at São Paulo, he collected the ball in midfield, looked up and whipped a beautiful, clever pass over the Ceará defence and into the path of his teammate, Iván Piris. *GOAL!*

Twenty minutes later, Casemiro dribbled the ball forward, looking for a pass, but when he got to thirty yards out, he decided to shoot instead. *BANG!* He hit a ferocious shot that dipped and swerved into the top corner.

Goooooooooooaaaaaaaaalllllllllllllll!!!!!!!!!!!!

Yes, he was big and powerful, but boy, could Casemiro play! Tackling, passing, dribbling, shooting – he made it all look so easy, and he didn't even look that excited. Instead, he just jogged away to the halfway line to hug his manager, Adilson Batista, and then get on with the game.

But just as everything was going so well, that's when the problems started. Maybe it was the exhaustion catching up with him after the World Cup, maybe it was his ego telling him that he had already 'made it' – or maybe it was a bit of both. Whatever the reason, Casemiro stopped playing like such a superstar, and São Paulo found themselves slipping further and further down the table: fourth, then fifth, then sixth, then seventh…

Nooooooooo, what was going wrong? What should they do? The São Paulo club President, Juvenal Juvêncio decided the answer was to sack Batista and bring in an experienced new manager. And that manager, Émerson Leão, decided the answer was to drop the team's most talented young midfielder. So, while Lucas and Willian José stayed in the starting line-up, Casemiro found himself sitting on the subs bench again.

'What am I doing here?' he groaned grumpily. 'It's not fair – I should be out there playing!'

He was young and still learning, so why weren't São Paulo giving him the support he needed and deserved? Was it because he was a defensive midfielder, rather than a flashy forward like Lucas? He was just experiencing a bad run of form, that was all. It happened to everyone, and he was sure that he would bounce back to his best soon.

But even when Casemiro did get to start against Athletico Paranaense, he didn't take his chance to shine by grabbing a great goal or an amazing assist. Instead, he received a yellow card early in the second half and Leão had to take him off before he got a red.

'Boooooooooooooooooooooooo!' the São Paulo supporters jeered.

Oh dear – how quickly things had changed for Casemiro. At the start of the season, he had been seen as one of the club's next big superstars, but now, months later, it was all about Lucas, who was being linked with moves to Chelsea and Real Madrid. Casemiro – who? He felt like he'd been forgotten already.

Maybe it was a case of: new season, new start? But no – when the 2012 campaign kicked off, it was the same story all over again. Casemiro did play some of the matches, but nowhere near as many as he wanted to, and with his confidence at a low, there were no more superstar performances. Even when São Paulo's other central midfielder, Wellington, suffered a serious injury, the coach didn't always call on Casemiro. Eventually, he became so frustrated that he started speaking out in public.

'They all praise me, they say I'm a great player, yet I never play,' Casemiro complained to the local journalists, which only made the situation even worse.

'Well, he's overweight and he doesn't work hard enough,' Leão claimed, and the São Paulo supporters took their manager's side.

'Who does that Casemiro think he is?' they asked. 'He's arrogant and he's only interested in the money.'

That wasn't true at all – the fans had got him all

wrong! Sometimes, he might seem arrogant, but that was only because Casemiro was a shy kid from the countryside who didn't feel comfortable talking to new people. And okay, maybe the fame might have gone to his head a little bit at first, but now all he wanted to do was play football for his team; that was way more important to him than the money!

It was too late to change their minds, though. The situation had got so bad that when São Paulo beat Club Atlético Tigre of Argentina to win the South American Cup, Casemiro wasn't even on the subs bench.

'Well done,' he congratulated his happy teammates, but he didn't feel like celebrating with them because he hadn't played any part in their victory.

What Casemiro really needed now was a fresh start and a change of scene. Would any of those exciting European clubs still be interested in signing him, though?

CHAPTER 10

A SURPRISING SIX MONTHS IN MADRID

Casemiro did join an exciting European club, in fact, but it wasn't a team in Italy or England, and it wasn't the kind of transfer everyone was expecting either. No, the midfielder went from not getting enough game-time at São Paulo to signing for Real Madrid... on loan!

The club's Head of Youth, Ramón Martínez, had been watching Casemiro's career closely for years, and in January 2013, he decided that it was the right time to step in. There was no doubt that the young Brazilian had the talent to become a top player, but things clearly weren't working out for him at São Paulo. In a new environment, however, hopefully

Casemiro could get back to his brilliant best, so why not bring him to Spain for six months and see?

'If the kid does well, we can sign him on a permanent deal in the summer,' Martínez explained to his coaches, 'and if he doesn't, then no harm done – he goes back to Brazil.'

It was a deal that suited everyone, really: Real Madrid, São Paulo, and especially Casemiro himself. This was the fresh start he needed, and what an opportunity to play for one of the world's biggest football clubs! Yes, it was only a six-month loan, but he didn't see it that way.

'I'm going to stay there and become a superstar,' Casemiro told his mum as he waved goodbye.

He wasn't walking straight into the Real Madrid first team, though, alongside superstars like Cristiano Ronaldo and Karim Benzema. On arrival, he was placed in the club's B team, called Castilla, who competed in the Spanish Segunda División. That's where all the club's promising young players started out.

'Welcome to the team!' the Castilla coach, Alberto Toril, greeted him on his first day at training.

Alberto had been warned about Casemiro's reputation for being difficult and not working very hard, but what he discovered was the exact opposite: a very professional player who got on well with everyone and helped make the team better.

'Hey thanks, that new kid is going to be great!' he admitted to Martínez.

'I told you!' the Head of Youth replied with a smile.

It took Casemiro a few matches to settle into life in the Segunda División, but once he did, he formed a strong midfield partnership with another young Brazilian called Fabinho, who was on loan from Rio Ave. Together, they took control of the game for Castilla and helped get the ball forward to the strikers, Jesé, Lucas Vázquez and Álvaro Morata.

'Thanks, you two!' Álvaro cheered as the team celebrated another goal together.

Once he felt more comfortable, Casemiro allowed himself to move up the pitch and join in on the attack. Against Alcorcón, he outjumped his marker and powered a header past the keeper. *1–0!*

Gooooooooooooaaaaaaaaalllllllllllllllll!!!!!!!!!!!!!

'Yesssssssssss!' Casemiro yelled as he leapt up to punch the air. Hurray, at last he was enjoying his football again!

And what a positive impact Casemiro was having. From sixteenth place in February, Castilla climbed all the way up to eighth by June.

'Can we keep him next season?' Toril pleaded with Martínez.

By then, however, Casemiro's talent had been spotted by the Real Madrid first team.

Ahead of their home match against Real Betis, manager José Mourinho had a midfield problem to deal with. Michael Essien was injured, Xabi Alonso was suspended, and he wanted to rest Sami Khedira for their Champions League semi-final. So, who else could play alongside Luka Modrić? What they needed was a holding midfielder, someone who would stay back and protect the defence, while Ronaldo, Benzema and Mesut Özil all pushed forward on the attack. And so after talking to Toril, Mourinho called for... Casemiro!

'The first team needs a midfielder,' the Castilla

coach said, 'so you'll be training with them this week.'

'Cool, thanks!' he replied excitedly.

Walking out onto the training pitch, Casemiro tried his best not to think about the fact that he was about to play with Ronaldo, Benzema, Özil and Kaká. 'Just treat it like any other football practice,' he told himself. This was a golden opportunity to impress the Real Madrid coaches, and to do that, he needed to stay calm and confident...

'Hey, he's a good player,' he heard Aitor Karanka say to Mourinho towards the end of the session.

The manager nodded. 'That's Casemiro. He's already played for Brazil and he's played a lot for São Paulo too.'

'Wow, so he really *does* know who I am,' Casemiro thought to himself, 'and he thinks I'm good!' Hopefully, that meant he might get to play a few minutes at least against Betis.

On the morning of the match, however, Mourinho told Casemiro to come to his hotel room. Uh-oh – was he in trouble, what had he done wrong? But no, the Real Madrid manager had good news, not bad news, to give him.

'Look,' he said, pointing at the team tactics board. 'You're in the starting line-up today.'

At first, Casemiro couldn't believe it. 'Really, me?' he wanted to ask and double-check, but there was no need – his name was right there on the list. What a lovely surprise!

'Who?' many of the Real Madrid fans wondered when they saw the teamsheet. 'Casemiro? I've never heard of him!' Was this just Mourinho trying to prove that he did give young players a chance?

No, not at all – Casemiro was the real deal, and he was determined to prove it. As he walked out at the Bernabéu to make his first-team debut, Real Madrid's new Number 38 did feel a little nervous, but he was also buzzing with excitement. This was it: his chance to show off his skills for one of the biggest clubs in the world.

'Let's do this!' Luka called out confidently.

Casemiro wasn't going to start trying lots of fancy tricks and flicks, though. No, that wasn't his style, and it wasn't his job; for today, he was focused on defending and keeping things nice and simple:

Blocks,

Tackles,

Interceptions,

Headers,

Short passes…

Well played, Case!

Just before half-time, his excellent debut got even better. Collecting the ball in midfield, Casemiro dribbled forward at speed. Then, when he was surrounded by Betis players, he passed it on to Mesut. Okay – over to you, attackers! Mesut played a lovely one-two with Karim, before sending the keeper the wrong way. *1–0!*

Hurray, what should he do now? As the new kid, Casemiro thought about just walking back to the halfway line, but he realised he had played his part in the goal, and so he turned around and joined in with the team celebrations.

'Great work!' cheered Mesut, giving him a double high-five.

At the final whistle, Real Madrid were 3–1 winners,

and Casemiro left the pitch feeling very proud of his debut performance. He had done everything his manager had asked of him, and more.

'A dream has come true for me,' he told the journalists. 'Playing my first game with Real Madrid is fantastic. My ambition is to get into the first team.'

Mourinho, however, had much higher ambitions than that for him. 'Case, you're going to be the best central midfielder in the world,' he declared.

CHAPTER 11

WATCHING, WAITING, LEARNING

As the 2012–13 season came to an end, Real Madrid had a big decision to make about Casemiro – should they sign him permanently, or send him back to São Paulo?

Well, after his brilliant debut against Betis, they agreed to sign him on a four-year deal, for a bargain fee of £6 million.

'I can't believe this is really happening!' Casemiro thought to himself while he smiled and held up the famous white shirt for the cameras.

This time, he didn't go back to the Real Madrid B team, but nor did he go straight into the starting line-up either. Instead, he was now one of five players fighting for only two places in midfield, and the others were all amazing and a lot more experienced: Sami, Luka, Xabi and Asier Illarramendi.

Wow, becoming a Real Madrid regular was going to be a real battle! Casemiro would have to be a lot more patient than he'd been at São Paulo, and spend a lot of time watching, waiting, and learning. He didn't mind that, though, because he was learning from some of the best midfielders in the game.

Sami was big, strong and brilliant at winning the ball back,

Luka was small but mighty, and a magician with the ball at his feet,

Xabi was hard-working, clever and incredible at passing, and so was Asier, only he was younger and fitter.

With each training session, Casemiro's sense of understanding and confidence grew, until eventually, he believed, 'Hey, I can do all that too!' He was powerful like Sami, he could be creative like Luka, he was smart like Xabi, and he was young like Asier.

'Pick me, pick me!' Casemiro said with his performances in practice, and the new Real Madrid manager, Carlo Ancelotti, agreed. When the new season kicked off, he selected Sami and Luka to start, and then brought on the club's promising new Brazilian to keep things calm and under control in the second half. No problem, Boss! Casemiro came on against Betis, Granada and Athletic Bilbao, and Real Madrid won all three matches.

'Well played, Case!'

As the season went on, however, he found himself stuck on the subs bench for game after game, if he was even selected in the matchday squad at all. It was a frustrating time for a young footballer who just wanted to play, but luckily there was a club legend around who encouraged him to keep going.

Zinedine Zidane was Ancelotti's assistant manager now, and he often stayed behind after training to do extra practice with Casemiro.

'You'll get your chance,' the Frenchman told him

when he felt like giving up. 'You just need to be ready to take it.'

Zidane was right; with Real Madrid competing for three different trophies, Ancelotti would need to rest his starting superstars sometimes. All Casemiro could do was wait for his manager's call and be ready to make the most of any opportunity.

In the Spanish league against Almería, he got to play the last twenty minutes and set up the fifth goal for Álvaro with a sensational long pass.

'Thanks, Case – what a ball!'

As a reward, a few days later, Ancelotti moved him into the starting line-up for their Champions League game against Galatasaray. For Casemiro, it was a new experience that he would never forget. What a feeling it was to walk out at the Bernabéu on a European night and stand there as the famous anthem played!

'This is where I belong,' Casemiro said to himself with a confident smile.

He was still buzzing as the match kicked off, but he didn't show it. Every time he got the ball, Casemiro controlled it and then moved it on calmly and accurately. Even when he knew opponents were racing in behind him, he took his time and never rushed his pass. He looked so composed out there, as if he'd been playing Champions League football for years.

And when there was defending to do, Casemiro was like a rock solid wall in front of the back four. Again and again, the Galatasaray midfielders tried to get past him, but he refused to be beaten. With blocks, tackles and interceptions, he kept winning the ball back for Real Madrid and then playing it forward to the attackers.

After sixty excellent minutes, Casemiro's European debut came to an end. As he jogged over to the touchline, high-fiving his fellow Brazilian Marcelo along the way, the Real Madrid supporters rose to their feet and clapped for their new midfield hero.

The Real Madrid manager was impressed too, and he decided to give Casemiro more chances in the Champions League.

In the Last 16 against Schalke, he came on for Xabi at half-time, and helped his team to win 3–1.

In the quarter-finals against Dortmund, he played the last fifteen minutes of both legs, and in the semi-final against Bayern Munich, he got ten minutes at the end, when the game was already won.

For the final against Atlético Madrid, however, he sadly didn't even make Ancelotti's matchday squad. Instead, the Real manager picked Asier as his back-up midfielder.

'Noooooooo!' Casemiro's heart sank when he heard the bad news. He was so disappointed to miss out on their biggest match of the season, but he tried his best not to show it.

'Next year,' he told himself as he congratulated his teammates on the trophy win. 'Next year, I'll get more game-time.'

Real also made it to the final of the Spanish Cup, where they beat Barcelona 2–1. This time, Casemiro did make it onto the pitch, but only for the last few minutes.

'Next year,' he told himself as he joined his teammates in a victory dive in front of the fans. 'Next year, I'll get more game-time.'

Two cup finals won, but only five minutes played – Casemiro had spent his first full season at Real Madrid watching, waiting and learning from the best, but next season, he really wanted more.

CHAPTER 12

MORE PLAYING TIME AT PORTO

During the summer of 2014, Xabi moved to Bayern Munich, but sadly his departure didn't mean that a space opened up for Casemiro in the Real Madrid midfield. Instead, the club had already signed a world-class alternative: German Toni Kroos.

Nooooo, not another new midfielder who would start ahead of him! Casemiro didn't know what to do. He was twenty-two years old now – was it time for him to give up on his Madrid dream and move on? He really didn't want to sit on the subs bench for another season, and Real didn't want that either. So, what about going away for a year on loan to another team where he would get more game-time?

That sounded like the best idea, but Casemiro wasn't ready to go back to Brazil. Were there any other European clubs that wanted him? He soon discovered he had plenty of options:

1) Casemiro could stay in Spain and spend the season at Sevilla. They had just won the UEFA Europa League, and their manager Unai Emery wanted him to replace their key midfielder Ivan Rakitić. Interesting!

2) He could head to Italy and join Inter Milan, just like he'd dreamed of doing during his early days at São Paulo. They were looking to rebuild their team after losing senior players like Javier Zanetti and Esteban Cambiasso, and he could be a key part of that. Exciting!

3) He could go to Portugal and play for Porto, alongside lots of other Brazilians, including his old Under-20 international teammates Danilo and Alex Sandro. Tempting!

'Come and play here with us – you'll love it!' they tried to persuade him.

At first, Casemiro's preferred choice was Option

1: staying in Spain with Sevilla. They were a top team, Emery was an amazing manager, and if he was playing in the same league, surely the Real Madrid coaches would be watching closely...

But after a short phone call with the new Porto manager, Julen Lopetegui, Casemiro changed his mind completely. 'I have to work with him,' he decided. What an inspiring man! He had ambitious plans for the club, and he wanted Casemiro to be a key part of them. Porto already had lots of attacking, creative midfielders – Óliver Torres, Rúben Neves, Evandro, Yacine Brahimi, Héctor Herrera – but what they were missing was a defensive midfielder who could sit deep and keep things calm and under control.

'That's me!' Casemiro thought to himself. Okay – now it was VERY tempting!

Plus, in Portugal they spoke the same language as in Brazil, and best of all, Porto would be playing in the Champions League. His mind was made up.

'Right, let's make this happen!' Casemiro told Real Madrid.

As soon as he arrived at Porto, Lopetegui handed him the Number 6 shirt and put him straight into the starting line-up. At last, plenty of playing time!

It was exactly what he needed, and the more minutes Casemiro got, the more his confidence grew. Yes, his main job was to protect the Porto defence, but that didn't mean he couldn't also help the attack sometimes. He scored his first league goal against Arouca with a powerful header, and he followed that up with two more:

A tap-in against Moreirense,

And a thunderbolt from thirty yards that left the Gil Vicente keeper with no chance.

Goooooooooooooooooooooaaaaaaaaaaaaaaaaallllllllllll llllllllllllllll!!!!!!!!!!!!!!!!!!!!

Casemiro threw his arms out wide and then jumped high into the air with his fists flying. It felt so good to be playing regular football again! He was learning lots from Lopetegui and improving every part of his skillset: tackling, passing, positioning, reading the game...

Finally, Casemiro was fulfilling his huge

potential and showing what a quality midfielder he could be, both in the Primeira Liga and in the Champions League.

In the last 16 against Swiss side FC Basel, Yacine gave Porto the lead in the fourteenth minute with a fantastic free kick. Hurray, what a start!

Anything he could do, however, Casemiro could do even better. Early in the second half, when the referee awarded them another free kick in a good area, the Brazilian grabbed the ball immediately. 'This one's mine,' he told his teammates.

'Okay, Case – go for it!'

Whereas Yacine had put lots of curl on his shot, Casemiro just went for pure power. After a long run-up, *BANG!* he blasted the ball up over the wall and it flew into the top corner of the net at astonishing speed. *3–0!*

Gooooooooooooooooooooaaaaaaaaaaaaaaaaalllllllllll llllllllllllllll!!!!!!!!!!!!!!!!!!!

Woah, what a strike! 'Come onnnnnnnnn!' Casemiro roared with joy as he slid towards the corner flag on his knees, followed by all of his shocked teammates.

Yessssss, Case – what a beauty!

That was one of the best free kicks I've ever seen!

'I really hope Real Madrid were watching that!' Casemiro thought to himself while he walked off the pitch after the final whistle. In the end, the club had agreed to sell him to Porto, but they still had the option to buy him back in the summer if they wanted to. He was certainly giving them something to think about with his superb performances.

Sadly, Porto's Champions League run came to an end in the quarter-finals, where they were beaten by Bayern Munich. But while Casemiro was disappointed, he wasn't too downhearted. They had battled hard against one of the best teams in the world, giving them two very tough games. What more could they have done? Nothing!

Although he finished the season without a trophy, Casemiro was focused on the positives. His move to Porto had worked out perfectly, with more playing time, more chances to shine, and lots more Champions League experience.

With 41 games, 4 goals and 3 assists, Casemiro could feel justly proud of his year, and suddenly, the football world was paying attention to him again.

In May, he was called up to the Brazil senior squad for the Copa América.

And in June, Real Madrid came calling, asking to bring him back to Spain.

CHAPTER 13

ZIDANE'S MAIN MAN IN MIDFIELD

Hurray, he was back! Casemiro couldn't wait to get going at Real Madrid again. It would be a new start for him, under a new manager. Rafa Benítez clearly rated him, otherwise why would he have asked to bring him back from Porto? And with both Sami and Asier gone, there was finally more game-time up for grabs in midfield.

Luka and Toni were still the first-choice starters, but they wouldn't play every minute, especially if other midfielders were performing well off the bench...

'I can do this!' Casemiro told himself with total confidence. During his season away at Porto, he had made major improvements to his game – he was now smarter, faster, and better on the ball. In the second game of the season, he came on and set up a goal for Gareth Bale with a brilliant, back-heel flick. *Olé!*

See, look what Casemiro could do! Now, when would he get the chance to play from the start? In early October, Benítez decided to switch to a three-man midfield for their big away match against local rivals, Atlético Madrid:

Luka, Toni, and in a slightly deeper, more defensive role… Casemiro!

That day, Real Madrid fought hard for a 1–1 draw, but in the games that followed, their new three-man midfield began to find a winning balance.

Real Madrid 3 Levante 0,

Celta Vigo 1 Real Madrid 3,

Real Madrid 3 Las Palmas 1…

Together, the three of them had a bit of everything: power, energy, calm, intelligence, and creativity. What a perfect midfield mix!

When it came to *El Clásico* against Barcelona, however, Benítez decided to switch back to his old formation. Out went Casemiro, and in came an extra attacker, James Rodríguez. Big mistake! With less protection in midfield, Barcelona ran riot, thrashing them 4–0.

'Booooooooooooooooooooooooooo!' The Real Madrid fans were furious and a few weeks later, Benítez was gone.

Oh dear, it was time for another new start for Casemiro, under another new manager, but who would it be? The answer was Zidane, the man who had been the assistant manager during his early days at the club! So, what would Zidane decide to do with Casemiro – play him or drop him? Within weeks, the answer was clear: Casemiro was there to stay. In fact, he was about to become Zidane's main man in midfield.

The Frenchman knew how important it was to have an excellent Number Six in your team. During his playing days at Real Madrid, Zidane had been part of an incredible group of superstars called 'The Galácticos', alongside Luís Figo, Ronaldo, Raúl and David Beckham. But having all of those attackers in one team would never have worked if it wasn't for one man: Claude Makélélé. While everyone else around him pushed forward, Makélélé stayed back and protected the defence, doing the work of three midfielders. Amazing! Zidane had been watching and working with Casemiro for years, and he was sure that Real Madrid had found their next excellent Number Six.

Wow! With his manager's full support, there was no stopping him now. Casemiro played the second half of the season like a real superstar.

In the Spanish league, he scored a last-minute winner against Las Palmas, and then helped his team to beat Barcelona away at the Nou Camp for the first time in years. Real Madrid even had to play the last ten minutes with ten men, after Sergio Ramos was sent off, but instead of panicking, they went up the other end and Ronaldo scored the winning goal!

Then it was over to Casemiro and the defence to keep out Lionel Messi, Neymar Jr and Luis Suárez until the final whistle blew...

'Yessssssssssssssss!' Casemiro cheered, dropping to his knees on the grass.

What a massive victory, and there were lots more to come, especially in the Champions League. With

Casemiro as the rock at the base of their midfield, Real Madrid went all the way, beating Roma in the Last 16, then Wolfsburg in the quarters, then Manchester City in the semis, to set up another local derby against Atlético, a repeat of the 2014 final.

But what a difference two years had made! Back then, Casemiro hadn't even made the subs bench as Real won 4–1 in extra-time. Now, he was one of the first names on Zidane's teamsheet.

As the 2016 Champions League final kicked off, Casemiro was out there on the pitch, playing in the biggest match of his career. What a feeling! The atmosphere was electric, it was all so exciting, but he had a crucial job to do for his team. So, while the other players around him pushed forward, Casemiro stayed back and protected the defence.

He rushed in to steal the ball before it reached the Atlético captain, Gabi. *Interception!*

He won the aerial battle against Fernando Torres and cleared the ball away. *Header!*

He calmly took the ball off Antoine Griezmann and then passed it to Toni. *Tackle!*

Yannick Carrasco tried and failed to find a way past him too. *Tackle!*

And so did Saúl Ñíguez. *Tackle!*

'Top work, Case!'

At half-time, Real were winning 1–0, thanks to a goal from Sergio Ramos, but just when it looked like they were going to hold on for the victory, Carrasco snuck in at the back post to equalise for Atlético. *1–1!*

Noooooooooooooooooooo! Casemiro couldn't believe it – after all their hard work! Oh well, they would just have to find another way to win…

But there were no more goals in the first ninety minutes, or in the thirty minutes of extra-time either. The final was heading all the way to… penalties!

'I'll take one,' Casemiro told his manager straight away, but at Real Madrid, he wasn't one of the top-five takers. So instead, he had to wait nervously on the halfway line and watch his teammates walk forward one by one:

Lucas Vázquez… scored!

Marcelo… scored!

Gareth… scored!

Sergio... scored!

And when Juanfran hit the post for Atlético, Cristiano took his chance to step up and be the hero. Hurray, Real Madrid were the Champions of Europe again!

When he saw the goal go in, Casemiro threw his arms in the air and raced around hugging as many teammates as he could. They had done it! And this time, he had played a key part in the victory, so he wanted to enjoy every minute of the celebrations.

Hala Madrid! Hala Madrid!

Campeones, Campeones, Olé! Olé! Olé!

Since his return from Portugal, Casemiro had completely turned his Real Madrid career around. Not only was he now Zidane's main man in midfield, but he was also a Champions League winner too. Yes, he had the medal to prove it, and he wasn't planning on taking it off. Ever.

CHAPTER 14

THE QUEST FOR THE QUADRUPLE

What do top footballers want to do once they've won one trophy? Relax? Far from it – they want to win lots more! That was certainly true of Casemiro and his Real Madrid teammates. For them, that Champions League win felt like just the beginning.

'Next season, we're going to win EVERYTHING!' Sergio declared, and he was serious about it.

Everything?! That would mean five trophies in one year for Real Madrid:

The UEFA Super Cup,

The FIFA Club World Cup,

The Spanish Cup,

The Spanish League,

And the Champions League.

Could they really win all five? With Cristiano, Karim and Gareth up front, and with Casemiro, Luka and Toni in midfield, anything was possible.

First up: the UEFA Super Cup final against the Europa League winners, Sevilla. Zidane rested most of his superstars for the match, but he kept Casemiro at the heart of the midfield. Why? Because there was no-one else like him!

That night, the Brazilian wasn't at his best, and neither were Real Madrid, but eventually they got the job done and the trophy won. This time, it was their defenders who came to the rescue. First, Sergio scored a last-minute equaliser, and then late in extra-time, right-back Dani Carvajal sprinted forward on an incredible solo run. *3–2!*

'Yesssssss!' Casemiro cheered at the final whistle with a big smile on his face, and then he jumped up on Dani's back as the celebrations began.

Hurrraaaaaaaaaaaaayyyyyyyyyyyyyyyyyyy!

Hala Madrid! Hala Madrid!

Campeones, Campeones, Olé! Olé! Olé!

They had won the UEFA Super Cup – what a way to kick off the new season! Right, now for the other four trophies...

But just as Casemiro was hitting top form again, disaster struck. In the Spanish league, he raced into a tackle with Espanyol's midfielder Pape Diop and got a hard kick around his left ankle.

Owwwwww!

At first, Casemiro tried to play on, but it was just too painful. Plus, what if he was making things worse? Eventually, he hobbled off the pitch, and Toni came on to take his place.

So, how serious was the injury? The team doctors did their tests straight away, and Casemiro kept his fingers crossed for good news. But it was bad news, unfortunately: he had fractured his fibula, and would be out for two months, if not longer.

'Nooooo, my team needs me!' Casemiro tried to argue, but there was nothing he could do, except rest and then recover as quickly as possible.

Get well soon, Case!

Without their main defensive midfielder, Real

Madrid found it much harder to win matches, but they kept their trophy dreams alive in the Spanish League and the Champions League.

'Well done, guys!' Casemiro cheered his teammates on from the stands, but it wasn't easy just sitting there, watching. He couldn't wait to be back out on the pitch with them – when would that be?

At last, in early December, he got his wish. He made his comeback as a sub against Barcelona, just in time for Real Madrid's trip to Japan for the FIFA Club World Cup. The chance to lift another trophy? Casemiro couldn't wait.

'We have to win this competition to finish the year well,' he announced at the press conference. 'When wearing the Real Madrid shirt, you have to always be focused and 100 per cent in the game.'

Injury, what injury? Casemiro was a man on a trophy mission. At the tournament, he didn't take things slowly; no, he played every minute for his team:

All ninety as they won 2–0 against Mexican side América in the semi-finals,

And then all 120 as they beat Kashima Antlers

4–2 in extra-time in the final, thanks to a Cristiano hat-trick.

First, they were Champions of Europe; now Real Madrid were the new Champions of the World! When the match ended, Casemiro took a deep, tired breath and then threw his arms up in the air. Rest and sleep could wait; it was time to party!

Hurrraaaaaaaaaaaaayyyyyyyyyyyyyyyyyy!

Hala Madrid! Hala Madrid!

Campeones, Campeones, Olé! Olé! Olé!

Three finals played, three trophies won – Casemiro was getting used to the fireworks and confetti now. And Real Madrid still had three more chances of silverware that season…

The Spanish Cup

Casemiro set up two goals to help Real beat Sevilla in the Last 16, but for the quarter-final against Celta Vigo, Zidane asked him to drop back into defence alongside Sergio.

No problem, Boss! Casemiro was happy to play anywhere to help out his team, but despite his best efforts, it was Celta who made it through to the semi-finals.

'Arggggh, we should have won that!' Casemiro groaned, kicking at the air in frustration.

It felt like a trophy lost, but at least there were two more up for grabs. Yes, Real's quest for the Quadruple was still on...

The Spanish League

Real had been top of the table for most of the season, but their big rivals Barcelona were only a few points behind, just waiting for them to slip up.

Slip up? No way! It was five long years since Real had last lifted the league title, and they were determined to do it again. They just had to keep going and keep finding ways to win.

Sergio was their hero against Real Betis, and then it was Casemiro's turn against Athletic Bilbao. When Cristiano's flick-on bounced down to him at the back post, he took his time to control the ball and then calmly passed it into the net. *2–1!*

Goooooooooooooaaaaaaaaalllllllllllllll!!!!!!!!!!!!

As Casemiro raced away towards the corner flag for a celebration knee-slide, his teammates were right behind him.

'Yesssss, Case!' Sergio cheered, giving him a high-five and a hug.

With each hard-fought victory, Real moved closer and closer to the trophy. They weren't going to let anything stop them, not even a 3–2 defeat to Barcelona. Three days later, they got straight back to winning ways, thrashing Deportivo La Coruña 6–2.

'Come on, we're nearly there now!' Casemiro shouted after smashing in the sixth goal.

In the end, the title race went all the way to the final day of the season, but Real never lost their nerve. With a 2–0 win over Málaga, they were crowned Champions of Spain.

Hurrraaaaaaaaaaaaayyyyyyyyyyyyyyyyyy!

Hala Madrid! Hala Madrid!

Campeones, Campeones, Olé! Olé! Olé!

The players danced around the pitch together in delight, while the fans celebrated in the stands above them. What a special moment, and what a special feeling!

'We did it, Case, and we couldn't have done it without you!' Zidane cried out happily, giving his midfield warrior a big hug.

Thanks, Boss! Winning the league had been a massive team effort, but when everyone gathered together for photos a few minutes later, there was one very important player missing.

'Hey, wait for me!' Casemiro called out suddenly and then slid across the grass like a superstar with a cheeky grin on his face, screaming 'Vamoooooooooooooooos!'

What a season Real were having! They had won the Treble – but now, could they go one step further and complete the Quadruple?

The Champions League...

CHAPTER 15

A(NOTHER) WINNING NIGHT IN WALES

3 June 2017, Millennium Stadium, Cardiff

The UEFA Super Cup, the FIFA Club World Cup, and the Spanish League title – could Real Madrid top off their remarkable season by lifting the Champions League trophy too? No team had won it twice in a row since AC Milan in the 1980s, but Real were now just one win away from that amazing achievement.

What a journey it had been to reach another Champions League final, and Casemiro had played a crucial role in every round.

In the Last 16 against Napoli, he had scored an absolute worldie, a booming thirty-yard volley that fizzed and swerved into the bottom corner. *GOAL!*

Woah, Case!

Then in the quarter-finals against Bayern Munich, with the game tied at 2–2, he had dribbled forward and delivered a teasing cross for Cristiano to head home. *ASSIST!*

Thanks, Case!

And in the semi-finals against Atlético Madrid, he had done it again, firing a bouncing ball across to Cristiano. *ASSIST!*

Yesssss, Case!

With Zidane's guidance and support, he had gone from a back-up to one of Real Madrid's most important, big-game players. So what could Casemiro come up with next, in the biggest game of all: the Champions League final?

Their opponents this time would be the Italian champions, Juventus, who were rock solid in defence, but also really dangerous in attack. Paulo Dybala had the skills, Mario Mandžukić had the strength, and Gonzalo Higuaín was one of the greatest goalscorers in the world.

The Real Madrid defence was definitely going to need Casemiro's protection, plus he would also have to help stop Miralem Pjanić and his old teammate Sami in midfield. It was going to be a very busy night of winning the ball back, but he was 110 per cent up for the challenge. This was what being a top professional footballer was all about.

'Vamoooooooooos!' Casemiro cheered in the huddle before kick-off.

As he expected, the first half was a fierce, tense and even contest. There were lots of tackles to win and loose passes to intercept – just the way Casemiro liked it! In the twentieth minute, Real took the lead when Cristiano finished off a great team move, then seven minutes later, Juventus equalised through Mandžukić. Game on!

With the score at 1–1, the final was perfectly set up for an exciting second half, but as the pressure increased, it was Real's superstars who shone the brightest. While the minutes ticked by, they relaxed, found their rhythm, and raised their game. It was no big deal; they had been here in the Champions

League final before, and so they knew what they needed to do. They just had to stay calm and believe in themselves and each other. As a team, they were unstoppable. No matter what the match was, they always seemed to find a way to win...

In the sixtieth minute, Toni's shot was cleared away by Alex Sandro, but only as far as... Casemiro!

'Leave it!' he called out to Luka; this one was his. In the Real Madrid midfield, Casemiro was usually the one who stayed back to defend, but once upon a time as a boy in Brazil, he had been a striker, and he still remembered how to shoot. He ran towards the ball as if he was racing into a tackle and then *BOOM!* he blasted it goalwards from thirty yards out.

'Ohhhhhhhhhhhhhhhhhhhhhhhhhh!' gasped the Real Madrid supporters, coaches and substitutes, rising from their seats in anticipation.

Was Casemiro's powerful strike on target? Yes.

Would Buffon have saved it? Probably, but the ball flicked up off Sami's leg and curled its way into the bottom corner, leaving the keeper with no chance. *2–1!*

Gooooooooooooaaaaaaaaalllllllllllllll!!!!!!!!!!!!

Casemiro didn't care about the big deflection; he was definitely still claiming his crucial Champions League final goal! He threw his arms out wide and raced towards the corner flag to celebrate in front of the fans. He was Real's hero again – another big game, another big-game moment!

'Yesssssss, Case!' his teammates cried out, throwing their arms around him.

The trophy wasn't theirs yet, though. At 2–1, anything could happen; the Real players needed to keep their concentration, and hopefully score another goal or two on the counter-attack.

No problem! A few minutes later, Luka won the ball back in midfield, played a one-two with Dani, and then crossed it in to Cristiano. *3–1!*

Okay – now they could really start thinking about that trophy! But just to make totally sure, Marco came on and scored another just before the final whistle. *4–1!*

It was all over; Real Madrid were the Champions of Europe again, and they had also completed the Quadruple!

'We did it!' Casemiro cheered, hugging Gareth and

lifting him high into the air. He was so proud to be a part of such a strong and successful team.

Later on, with his winner's medal around his neck, Casemiro sat at the front of the stage and roared while Sergio lifted the trophy above his head and into the confetti-filled Cardiff sky.

Hurrraaaaaaaaaaaaayyyyyyyyyyyyyyyyyy!

Hala Madrid! Hala Madrid!

Campeones, Campeones, Olé! Olé! Olé!

What a night, and what a year! Four major trophies, plus back-to-back Champions League final wins – it was far beyond even Casemiro's wildest football dreams. How could life possibly get any better than this?

CHAPTER 16

THREE IN A ROW!

During the summer of 2017, Real Madrid decided not to make any major new signings. Why mess with a winning team?

The players knew that they couldn't just sit back and relax, though. No, to keep lifting top trophies, they had to keep improving. That's why Casemiro worked so hard, every single day:

In the gym to get stronger,

And on the training field to get fitter.

Sitting in ice baths to recover faster,

And watching video clips to think smarter.

Yes, even away from the pitch, Casemiro was always listening and always learning.

'Can't you just stop and switch off for a week?' his wife, Anna, asked him during the summer break, but sadly the answer was no. Football was his life!

As a young player back at São Paulo, perhaps his attitude hadn't always been the best, but since his breakthrough at Real Madrid, Casemiro had become the ultimate professional. And look what a difference it had made to his performances! He was one of the best midfielders in the world now, and he was determined to stay there at the top, winning lots more tournaments…

The UEFA Super Cup again? *Tick!*

This time, Real Madrid faced Premier League giants Manchester United in the final.

'Manchester United!' Casemiro thought back to his first trip to Old Trafford, aged fifteen, to play for São Paulo in the Nike Cup. What an experience! The club would always have a special place in his heart for that reason, but once he was out on the football pitch, winning always came first.

Despite all of Real Madrid's attacking talents, it was

actually their defensive midfielder who turned out to be the danger man against Manchester United.

In the tenth minute, Casemiro's powerful strike flew just wide of the post. *Nearly!*

Five minutes later, his diving header crashed back off the crossbar. *So unlucky!*

But the Brazilian wasn't giving up. Another ten minutes later, he burst into the Manchester United box again, and this time, he slid in and scored. *1–0!*

Goooooooooooaaaaaaaaalllllllllllllllll!!!!!!!!!!!!

What a cool, calm finish! After a quick check for an offside flag, Casemiro just jogged away towards the corner flag like it was no big deal, like he scored in big European finals all the time.

'Yesssss, Case – you hero!' Marcelo cried out, throwing his arms around his very important teammate.

At the final whistle, the match finished 2–1 to Real Madrid. Another trophy won – what a way to start the new season! And after a fun night of celebrations, Casemiro and his teammates moved straight onto their next challenge...

The Spanish Super Cup? *Tick!*

Defeating their big rivals Barcelona? No problem! Real Madrid cruised to victory, beating them in both legs to lift the trophy for the first time since 2012. Zidane was even able to give Casemiro a rare rest in the home game at the Bernabéu. But Casemiro still came on for the last thirty minutes, though, and naturally stayed for the celebrations afterwards.

Campeones, Campeones, Olé! Olé! Olé!

Medals collected, trophy lifted, happy memories made. Okay, and onto the next one…

The FIFA Club World Cup again? *Tick!*

Real Madrid weren't at their best at the tournament in Abu Dhabi, but they still battled their way to glory. With narrow victories over Al-Jazira and then Brazilian club Grêmio, they claimed yet another trophy. Wow, they had already won another Treble, and it wasn't even Christmas time yet!

Did the winning feeling fade for Casemiro, with each final that he won? Quite the opposite – he remained as excited as ever. When Cristiano scored the goal against Grêmio, Casemiro raced over to him at top speed and jumped up so high in the huddle that he fell over and almost hurt himself!

So after a sensational 2017, what could Real Madrid achieve in 2018? By the end of January, they had been knocked out of the Spanish Cup, and in the Spanish League, they were 16 points behind the leaders Barcelona. That only left one last trophy up for grabs, and it was the biggest of them all:

The Champions League again? *Tick!*
Yes, *Los Blancos* successfully made it three in a row – incredible! No club had achieved that since Bayern Munich in the 1970s, but Real Madrid were now a winning machine. As hard as the other top European teams tried, none of them could stop them:
Not Borussia Dortmund, with Pierre-Emerick Aubameyang and Christian Pulisic,
Not PSG, with Neymar Jr and Kylian Mbappé,
Not Juventus, with Dybala and Higuaín,
Not even Bayern Munich, with Robert

Lewandowski, Franck Ribéry and Arjen Robben.

The champions of France, Italy and Germany – Real Madrid had beaten them all, on the way to another Champions League final! There, they faced Liverpool, whose fantastic front three had been on fire all season: Sadio Mané, Roberto Firmino and Mohamed Salah.

'Bring it on!' the Real Madrid players responded to the challenge. Sergio and his fellow defenders would deal with Salah and Mané, and who would mark Firmino, the 'false nine' who liked to drop deep? That was Casemiro's job, and his teammates trusted him to keep any attacker quiet.

After sixty minutes, the game was still tied at 1–1, but in the end, Real blew them away with their big-game experience. Pressure, what pressure? As always, Real's superstars stayed calm, raised their game, and found a way to win.

Casemiro carried the ball forward from midfield and then chipped a long pass out to Marcelo on the left wing, who crossed it into the box. The ball was behind Gareth, but instead of just leaving it, he went for an outrageous overhead kick. *2–1!*

Unbelievable, it was one of the greatest goals Casemiro had ever seen! He raced over to the corner flag, roaring with passion, and then jumped on top of the big pile of Real Madrid players. Boy, he loved playing for this extra-special team!

With ten minutes to go, Gareth scored again with a swerving shot that slipped through the Liverpool keeper's gloves. Game over, Real Madrid were the Champions of Europe yet again!

Hurrrraaaaaaaaaaaaaayyyyy!

When the final whistle blew, Casemiro fell to his knees near the halfway line. They had done it; three in a row. What an amazing achievement!

'I am very happy because of the history we are writing,' he said to the journalists with a smile. 'We need to congratulate everybody. What we are doing is not normal.'

CHAPTER 17

BATTLING FOR BRAZIL

Casemiro didn't have long to relax and enjoy Real's European glory, though. Soon, he was heading off to represent his country... at the 2018 World Cup! Yes, finally, his childhood dream was coming true, and he was following in the footsteps of Ronaldo and Ronaldinho, his heroes from 2002. Casemiro had already won the World Cup once before, with the Brazil Under-20s in 2011 – could he now do it again with the senior team?

'I can't wait for this!' he told his old friends Neymar Jr and Philippe as they travelled together to Russia.

Despite making his Brazil debut way back in 2011, Casemiro was still yet to reach twenty-five caps for his country. That's because for years, the national team managers had selected other defensive midfielders instead.

Paulinho, Fernandinho and Luis Gustavo had been Luiz Felipe Scolari's main men at the 2014 World Cup in Brazil, which ended in an embarrassing 7–1 defeat to Germany in the semi-finals. Then a year later at the Copa América, Dunga had picked Fernandinho, Fred and Elias, leaving Casemiro stuck on the bench.

Luckily, everything had changed in 2016, when Tite took over. In his very first match in charge against Ecuador, Brazil's new manager chose Casemiro at the base of the midfield, and it had stayed that way ever since. While forwards Neymar Jr, Philippe, Gabriel Jesus and Willian all attacked with freedom, Casemiro stayed back, protecting the defence and winning the midfield battle, just like he did for Real Madrid.

Hurray, at last the Brazil team had the balance that they'd been looking for! With Casemiro in midfield, they hadn't lost any of their last twenty matches. No wonder they were now one of the favourites to win the 2018 World Cup.

The players weren't getting carried away, though. No, they knew that anything could happen in a nerve-wracking, knock-out competition. There would be no easy wins at the World Cup, only hard-fought battles, and that's why Brazil's holding midfielder was going to be so crucial.

'Come on, Case – let's do this!'

A 1–1 draw against Switzerland wasn't the start they were hoping for, but they soon found their rhythm and balance after that:

2–0 against Costa Rica,

2–0 against Serbia,

And 2–0 against Mexico in the Round of 16.

'Vamoooooooos!' the Brazil players celebrated together after the final whistle.

They weren't always playing the beautiful, samba-style football that their fans expected, but hey, they were getting the job done. They looked solid at the back, and they were scoring goals in attack – surely winning matches was the most important thing?

Going into their quarter-final against Belgium, though, Brazil had a major problem – one of their most important players was suspended. No, not Neymar Jr, or Philippe – Casemiro! He had picked up his second yellow card of the tournament against Mexico, which meant he would now miss the next match. Noooooooooooo, what were they going to do without their best defensive midfielder?

Unfortunately, the answer was: lose. First, his replacement, Fernandinho, flicked a header into his own net, and then Romelu Lukaku and Kevin De Bruyne ripped through their defence with ease. Without Casemiro's calming presence, Brazil's midfield just couldn't cope.

'Arggggh, I really wish I was out there!' he winced, watching from the stands. It was so horrible to see his team struggle like this and not be able to help them.

Brazil were down 2–0 at half-time – was their World Cup over? In the second half, they did their best to fight back. Philippe set up Renato Augusto to keep the dream alive, and then with seconds to go, it looked like Neymar Jr had scored an equaliser, but no, Thibaut Courtois made a sensational save.

Ohhhhhhhhhhhhhhhhhhhhhhhhhh!

Now, Brazil's World Cup really was over. Despite their high hopes, they were heading home early.

Casemiro was devastated, of course, but after the game when the media asked about Fernandinho, he defended his teammate fiercely. 'He's a great player and we have faith in him,' he said. 'When we lose, everybody loses. When we win, everybody wins.'

It was as simple as that. Brazil would just have to work together to come back even stronger for their next competition: the 2019 Copa América.

As the tournament hosts, Brazil were the favourites to lift the trophy, but it was very nearly the same sad story as the 2018 World Cup. Again, Casemiro picked up two yellow cards and had to miss their quarter-final match, and again, the team looked lost without him. This time, however, they battled their way to penalties and managed to beat Paraguay in the shoot-out.

Phew, Brazil were through to the semi-finals! There, they would face their big rivals Argentina, but at least they would have their best defensive midfielder back to help keep Messi quiet. The players, the coaches, the supporters – everyone felt more confident when

Casemiro was in the team.

Once the match kicked off, he came out battling for Brazil.

Header! Casemiro jumped up and beat Sergio Agüero to the high ball.

Block! He threw his body bravely in front of Rodrigo De Paul just as he was about to play a pass.

Interception! He read Messi's mind and stole the ball off him.

Tackle! As Ángel Di María dribbled towards goal, he raced across to deal with the danger.

There were a few fouls too, but Casemiro couldn't help that. It was all part of his job of protecting the defence.

'Thanks, Case!'

When the final whistle blew, Brazil were the winners, thanks to goals from Gabriel Jesus and Firmino, but could they have done it without the hard, dirty work of Casemiro in midfield? No – no way!

'Now, we've got to win the trophy,' he told his teammates determinedly.

And Brazil did, beating Peru 3–1 in the final.

Hurray, they were the Champions of South America for the first time since 2007! Afterwards, the whole squad celebrated together in front of 60,000 home fans at the Maracanã Stadium.

Vamooooossssssssssssss!

CAMPEÕES! CAMPEÕES!

For Casemiro, it was yet another glorious, trophy-winning night, but this one did feel extra-special. After achieving so much success with his club, Real Madrid, it was fantastic to finally do the same with his country. He was so proud to play football for Brazil, and now, together with his teammates, he had helped bring joy to the nation again.

CHAPTER 18

REAL WITHOUT RONALDO

Just when things were going really well with Brazil, Casemiro found himself facing a new challenge at Real Madrid. Why? Because their dream team had broken up!

Well, sort of. Just days after their Champions League final victory over Liverpool, their manager Zidane had announced that he was leaving, and there were rumours that he might not be the only one. Was Ronaldo about to wave goodbye too?

'I don't see him playing outside of Real Madrid,' Casemiro had said straight after the final, but sadly, he was wrong about that. Weeks later, Cristiano had signed for Italian club Juventus.

Nooooo, their superstar striker was gone! It really felt like the end of a glorious era. What next? Real Madrid still had Karim and Gareth in attack and Casemiro, Toni and Luka in midfield, but would they be able to carry on winning without Cristiano?

The first test came in the UEFA Super Cup final against Atlético Madrid. With twenty minutes to go, Real were 2–1 up and heading towards another trophy, but their local rivals fought back and won it 4–2 in extra-time.

Oh dear, Real had lost a final for the first time since 2013! Had they lost their winning edge when they lost their superstar striker?

'Of course, we missed Cristiano Ronaldo, this is natural,' Casemiro admitted afterwards, but he was confident that his team could adapt and find a new way to win.

It took some time for Real Madrid to get used to life without Ronaldo, but eventually, they managed to move on and move forward. Apart from lifting the FIFA Club World Cup again, 2018–19 had been a season to forget, but 2019–20? It was going to be great!

Instead of signing an expensive, experienced striker to replace Cristiano, Real had given the star role to Karim and brought in three of South America's most exciting young attackers to play alongside him:

Federico Valverde, an energetic midfielder from Uruguay, and Vinicius Jr and Rodrygo, two speedy, skilful wingers from Brazil.

'Bem-vindo!' Casemiro greeted his fellow countrymen with a warm, friendly smile. As one of the club's senior players now, he was there to help the young South Americans settle in as quickly as possible.

As well as the new signings, Real also had their old manager back. Yes, after a year away, Zidane had returned to lead them to lots more trophies. Hurray! Casemiro couldn't wait to work with him again.

'For the team, Zidane never left,' he told the Spanish media.

So, what could they win together this time? In the Champions League, Real were beaten by Pep Guardiola's Manchester City in the Last 16, but in the Spanish League, they battled Barcelona all the way for the title.

While Karim was the team's top scorer, the Brazilians certainly played their part. The youngsters were finding their feet and Casemiro was still as important as ever, in defence but also in attack.

Against Levante, Vini raced up the right wing and crossed the ball into the middle for Casemiro to score. *3–0!*

Goooooooooooooooooooooaaaaaaaaaaaaaaaaaalllllllllllllll llllllllllllll!!!!!!!!!!!!!!!!!!!!

Against Osasuna, Vini scored the first goal and Rodrygo scored the second, after a beautiful long pass from Casemiro.

'Vamoooossssssssssssss!' they celebrated together.

In January, Real Madrid won the Spanish Super Cup. Meanwhile, in the league, they were still tied with Barcelona at the top of the table, on forty points each. Ooooof, what an exciting title race! Every win mattered. Next up for Real: Sevilla. A big game like that called for a big-game player, and with Karim on the bench, someone else was going to need to step up instead…

Casemiro spent most of the match sitting deep, protecting the defence like usual, but early in the second half, he moved forward and won the ball back in a really good position on the edge of the Sevilla penalty area.

Ohhhhhhhhhhhhhhhh...

Casemiro could see Vini in the middle waiting for the cross, but instead he carried the ball forward himself, using his strength to hold off two defenders. As the goalkeeper rushed out towards him, he had a quick decision to make: pass or shoot? Casemiro went for the second option, lifting the ball over the diving keeper with a cheeky little chip. *1–0!*

Goooooooooooaaaaaaaaallllllllllllllll!!!!!!!!!!!!

'Yessssss, Case!' his teammates cheered while they chased after him.

Sevilla equalised a few minutes later, but just like during their glory days with Cristiano, Real found a way to win. Lucas Vázquez curled a brilliant cross into the six-yard box, and who was there in the striker's position to meet it with a powerful, leaping header? Yes, Casemiro!

Goooooooooooaaaaaaaaallllllllllllllll!!!!!!!!!!!!

'VAMOOOOOOOSSSSSSSSS!' he roared in front of

the Real Madrid fans. Soon, the league title would be theirs; he was going to make sure of that.

When the season had to stop suddenly in March 2020 due to the coronavirus, Real were two points behind Barcelona. But when football restarted three months later, they returned on fire, winning game after game after game:

Real Madrid 2 Eibar 0,

Real Madrid 3 Valencia 0,

Real Sociedad 1 Real Madrid 2,

Real Madrid 2 Real Mallorca 0,

Espanyol 0 Real Madrid 1…

In a very close match, it was Casemiro who made the difference yet again. Just before half-time, he raced on to Karim's back-heel pass and smashed the ball past the Espanyol keeper.

'Yessssssssssssss!' he yelled as he leapt and punched the air. It felt so strange playing in silent stadiums with no supporters there to cheer them on, but nothing was going to stop them from achieving their goal.

…Real Madrid 1 Getafe 0,

Athletic Bilbao 0 Real Madrid 1,

Real Madrid 2 Alavés 0,
Granada 1 Real Madrid 2,
Real Madrid 2 Villarreal 1…

Hurray, they had done it; they had won the Spanish League title, their first major trophy without Cristiano!

At the final whistle, Casemiro threw his tired arms up in the air and then took a moment to catch his breath. All that effort, all season long – but it had been worth it for this, this fantastic winning feeling!

'*Campeones, Campeones, Olé! Olé! Olé!*' the Real players sang together again and again, their words echoing around the empty stadium, but it was all being filmed for the fans watching and celebrating in their homes.

CHAPTER 19

ANCELOTTI'S FIREFIGHTER

'Ancelotti?' Casemiro wondered to himself when he heard the news. 'Again?'

After a disappointing 2020–21 season without winning a single trophy, Zidane had decided to leave Real Madrid once more, which meant that the team needed a new manager. But instead of offering the job to someone young and promising, the club president Florentino Pérez had gone back to another old coach, Italian Carlo Ancelotti.

Ancelotti had previously managed Real Madrid between 2013 and 2015, during Casemiro's first years at the club. Back then, the Brazilian had spent most of his time on the subs bench, but a lot had changed since then. Now, he was one of the best defensive midfielders in the world, plus one of Real Madrid's most important players, and Ancelotti couldn't wait to work with him again.

'Perhaps Casemiro could've played more minutes during my first stint at the club,' his manager admitted as he handed him a new four-year deal. 'I've spoken to him about this and I told him that I may have been wrong with that. Right now, he's an essential player for this side.'

Thanks, Boss! While Casemiro would miss being Zidane's main man in midfield, he was looking forward to a fresh start as Ancelotti's firefighter. Sitting deep, dealing with danger, protecting the defence – yes please! Casemiro simply loved saving the day for his team.

When the 2021–22 season kicked off, Real got off to a flying start. In the Spanish League, they began by thrashing Alavés 4–1, and thanks to win after win after win, they stayed there at the top of the table until in late April, the title was theirs.

Campeones, Campeones, Olé! Olé! Olé!

The next day on social media, Casemiro posted smiling pictures of himself holding the trophy with Toni and Luka. The three of them were great friends, both on and off the football pitch, and even after so many years in the same team, they still loved playing together. Oh, and winning together, of course!

'The Bermuda Triangle,' Casemiro wrote underneath the photos. That was the new nickname that Ancelotti had given to his amazing midfield trio. What did he mean? Well, the Bermuda Triangle was a mysterious place where lots of planes and ships had disappeared, and he said that the same thing happened to the ball when Casemiro, Toni and Luka were together in the Real Madrid midfield. It magically disappeared!

So, the Spanish League title, plus the Spanish Super Cup – but there was still one more trophy up for grabs for Real Madrid, because they were through to the Champions League final yet again!

What an unbelievable journey it had been. Again and again, Real seemed on the verge of being knocked out, but each time, they somehow turned things around and found a way to win.

In the Round of 16, they had fought back from 2–0 down to beat Messi, Mbappé and Neymar Jr's PSG by 3–2.

¡Hala Madrid!

And the quarter-final against Chelsea had been even more of a rollercoaster ride. After winning the first leg 3–1, Real found themselves 4–3 down in the second leg with only fifteen minutes to go. But back they came to win 5–4 in extra-time!

¡Hala Madrid!

Surely, the semi-final against Manchester City couldn't be any more exciting than that? Wrong! As the second leg at the Bernabéu entered injury time, City were winning 5–3 and their fans were starting to look ahead to the Champions League final.

Real Madrid's superstars weren't giving up, though. Why would they? The Champions League was *their* competition! If any team could fight back, they could.

First, Karim volleyed the ball across for Rodrygo to score. *5–4!*

Then, Dani crossed the ball in and Rodrygo headed

it home. *5–5!*

Wow, two goals in two minutes – the game was going to extra-time! By then, Casemiro had been taken off to bring on an extra attacker, but watching from the subs bench, he had full belief in his team. Of course, they could win this...

In the ninety-fifth minute, Rodrygo fired the ball across to Karim, who was fouled as he burst into the box. Penalty! There was no way Karim was going to miss from the spot. *6–5!*

That was it. Mission impossible: complete!

¡Hala Madrid!

After a night of joyful celebrations, Casemiro sent a message out to his fans on social media: 'TO PARIS!'

That's where the Champions League final would be played, and there, they would face the team that they'd beaten back in 2018: Liverpool. The Reds were in great form and out for revenge, but in a big European final, you could never rule out Real Madrid. Especially not when Ancelotti's firefighter was there, ready to save the day for his team.

Vamoooooosssssssssssss!

Sadio Mané turned and tried to race away towards goal, but TACKLE! Casemiro slid in to win the ball back brilliantly.

Luis Díaz dribbled infield, away from Éder Militão, but TACKLE! Casemiro was there to stop him.

Trent Alexander-Arnold lined up a long-range shot, but BLOCK! Casemiro bravely threw his body in front of the ball.

Yesssssss, Case!

He was like a wall in front of the Real Madrid defence, and as hard as they tried, Liverpool were finding it really hard to break through. Even when they did, they then had to get past Éder and David Alaba behind him, plus Thibaut Courtois in goal. Impossible!

Meanwhile, at the other end, Real were starting to create chances of their own. Just before half-time, Karim had a goal ruled out for offside, and then in the sixtieth minute, they launched a flowing move from back to front. Luka passed the ball to Dani, who played it inside to Casemiro, who looked up and sprayed it out wide to Federico on the right wing. He dribbled forward and then from just inside the penalty area, he fired a dangerous ball across the six-yard box. It fizzed through the legs of Virgil van Dijk, then past Karim and Ibrahima Konaté, past Alexander-Arnold, and all the way through to Vini at the back post. *1–0!*

But wait, was he offside? No, after a long VAR check, the goal was given – Real were winning!

'Yessssssss!' Casemiro cried out, clenching his fists with passion.

Right, now they just had to stay strong and hold on. To do that, Real were going to need their defensive midfielder more than ever.

Mo Salah attempted to slip a pass through to Mané, but INTERCEPTION! Casemiro got himself in the way.

Diogo Jota made a sudden burst into the box, but BLOCK! Casemiro was right there beside him.

Mané tried to escape up the wing, but TACKLE! Casemiro wasn't going to let that happen.

Jota flicked the ball on towards Roberto Firmino, but CLEARANCE! Casemiro was there to boot it high and away.

Yessssssss, Case!

He wasn't the only Real Madrid hero, though; it was one big team effort. Éder and David were both excellent in defence, while Thibaut was magnificent in goal, making supersave after supersave. At last, the final whistle blew – it was all over, and they had done it. They were the Champions of Europe yet again!

¡HALA MADRID!

Later on, once Marcelo had lifted the trophy, Casemiro posed for more smiling pictures with Toni and Luka out on the pitch. What an amazing midfield trio they were! With one hand, they held the trophy, and with the other, they held up the number five. Why five fingers? One for each of their Champions League wins together.

CHAPTER 20

MOVING TO MANCHESTER

After winning five Champions League trophies, three Spanish league titles and three FIFA Club World Cups, was there really anything left for Casemiro to achieve at Real Madrid? During the summer of 2022, he had a big decision to make: did he want to stay in Spain for the rest of his career, or was it time to move on and tackle a new challenge somewhere else?

He was thirty years old now, Toni was thirty-two, and Luka was thirty-six, so the club had already started preparing for life without their amazing midfield trio. First, Fede Valverde had joined the first team back in 2018, then exciting youngster Eduardo Camavinga had arrived in 2021, and now fellow

Frenchman Aurélien Tchouaméni was about to join him. Tchouaméni was twenty-two and a defensive midfielder, just like Casemiro – was he there to take his place straight away? Hmmm, maybe it was time to move on...

Meanwhile, over in England, Manchester United were attempting to solve their major midfield problems. Their new manager Erik ten Hag had already brought in playmaker Christian Eriksen, and now he was determined to sign a new Number Six – someone who could protect the defence but also help launch the team's attacks.

At first, United's top target was Dutchman Frenkie de Jong, but when he decided that he didn't want to leave Barcelona, ten Hag turned to other options: Declan Rice, Jude Bellingham, Youri Tielemans, Rúben Neves...

'What about Casemiro?' the United scouts wondered.

Okay, so Casemiro wasn't a young player anymore, but the Real Madrid midfielder was a world-class winner, and that's what United needed. Plus, he was a hard-working pro with years of experience at the highest level. Surely, it was worth a try?

A move to Manchester United – very interesting! Casemiro had loved the club ever since his first trip to Old Trafford, aged fifteen. It was a massive team with lots of history, just like Real Madrid, but since Sir Alex Ferguson's retirement in 2013, they had struggled to win trophies. Could he help change that with his big-game know-how? It would certainly be an exciting new challenge...

Casemiro sent a message to his Brazil teammate Fred, who was already in Manchester. 'Maybe I will come to United,' he wrote.

Really? That would be brilliant! Fred replied straight away: 'You need to come here today, right now!'

And Fred wasn't the only one United player who urged him to join the club. Casemiro also got a phone call from his old Real Madrid teammate Raphaël Varane, who did his best to convince him.

'You'll love it here,' he said, 'and the fans will love you, Warrior!'

The more Casemiro talked to his friends and family about it, the more tempting a move to Manchester sounded, until eventually, his mind was made up. Of course, he was going to miss Madrid so much, but it felt like the right time to try something new.

'Sorry, Boss, but I want to go,' he told Ancelotti, who accepted his decision with a heavy heart, and so did Luka and Toni.

'Good luck, Case!' they said. 'You've been the best bodyguard in the world!'

Now, the two clubs just needed to agree a transfer fee and get the deal done…

That took time, however, and so when the 2022–23 Premier League season kicked off, Casemiro was still a Real Madrid player. Oh well – it gave him a chance to watch Manchester United's first few matches and find out more about his new teammates and ten Hag's tactics. What he saw, however, was very worrying indeed:

Manchester United 1 Brighton and Hove Albion 2, Brentford 4 Manchester United 0…

Two games, two defeats – oh dear, what a

disastrous start to the season! What on earth was going on? The whole team looked an absolute mess, but especially the defence and midfield.

Some players might have watched that thrashing by Brentford, and thought, 'No thanks!', but not Casemiro.

'Tell United to stay calm,' he told his agent confidently. 'Tell them I'll fix this.'

Really? Could he do that? Was he really the right the man for the job? When Casemiro finally arrived at the club, lots of fans had their doubts about him, especially due to his age.

'What a waste of money – £70 million for a thirty-year-old?'

'Bastian Schweinsteiger, Alexis Sánchez, and now this guy – why do we keep signing all these big players who are past it?'

'Has he really got the pace for the Premier League? I don't think so...'

Casemiro wasn't going to let the talk affect him, though; he loved proving people wrong. He was fully focused on achieving the goals that he had set out at his first press conference:

'I can't wait to produce on the pitch and help out my teammates to win games and to go on to win trophies.'

That was the plan, and the other Manchester United players were delighted to have him there. From his very first training session, he began changing the atmosphere at the club with his hard-working attitude.

'Come on, Case – let's get winning!' his new captain, Bruno Fernandes, cheered.

Casemiro wasn't in the squad for the 2–1 victory over Liverpool, but he did come on as a late sub in their next match against Southampton. When he entered the pitch, United were already winning 1–0, so his job was simple: sit deep, protect the defence, and keep things calm.

No problem! Casemiro took charge of the midfield, winning headers and tackles, and playing quick, simple passes. Then, late in injury time, Southampton got one last chance to score. Sékou Mara's overhead kick was saved by David de Gea, and the rebound fell to Lyanco. But as the defender went to shoot, BLOCK! Casemiro came in and cleared the danger.

Hurrrraaaaaaaaaaaaaaayyyyy!

He had only played ten minutes, and he was already a fans' favourite!

Casemiro carried on playing the super-sub role for the next few weeks, until finally ten Hag decided that he was ready to make his full debut. In the fourth minute, he took too long on the ball and Everton scored, but United soon fought back, and who set up the winning goal with a brilliant tackle and pass? Yes, Casemiro!

He was loving life in the Premier League, and he was fixing Manchester United's midfield problems, just like he'd promised. Suddenly, the whole team looked more balanced, more confident, and more determined to win, no matter what.

Away at Chelsea, United gave away a late penalty, but they didn't just give up as they had in the past. Instead, they kept calm and pushed forward on the attack. From the left, Luke Shaw curled a teasing cross into the box, and up jumped Casemiro to power an amazing header over the keeper and in off the post. *1–1!*

Goooooooooooooooooooaaaaaaaaaaaaaaaaalllllllllllll llllllllllllllll!!!!!!!!!!!!!!!!!!!!

'Yesssssssssssssssssssssssssssssssssssss!' Casemiro roared as he celebrated in front of the United fans. What an impact – he was a club hero already!

CHAPTER 21

WORLD CUP PENALTY PAIN

Just as Casemiro was starting to feel settled in the Manchester United midfield, the club season came to a stop. Why? Because it was time for the players to represent their countries at the 2022 World Cup in Qatar!

Would Brazil perform better and progress further than they had in Russia four years earlier? Casemiro was feeling confident. 'There's no doubt our options are much greater than in 2018,' he said at a press conference, 'and not only because time has passed, and we are more mature.'

In attack, as well as Gabriel Jesus and Neymar Jr, they also now had Richarlison, Raphinha, Casemiro's old Real Madrid teammates, Vinicius Jr and Rodrygo, and his new teammate at Manchester United, Antony.

In midfield, as well as Casemiro and Fred, they also now had Fabinho, Lucas Paquetá and Bruno Guimarães.

And in defence, as well as Marcelo and Thiago Silva, they also now had Marquinhos, Danilo, Alex Sandro and Éder Militão.

What a squad, what an exciting mix of youth and experience! On paper, their team looked unbeatable, but could they go all the way and win the World Cup? Challenge accepted!

In their opening game against Serbia, Brazil had lots of the ball, but it took them a long time to break through and score. At last, after sixty-two minutes, Neymar Jr danced through the defence and set up Vinicius Jr. His shot was saved but the rebound fell to Richarlison. *1–0!*

Phew! As he raced over to the corner flag to join his teammates, Casemiro's main feeling was relief. Brazil were off the mark at the World Cup! The players began to relax a bit after that, and ten minutes later,

Richarlison produced a piece of pure samba skill. Flicking the ball up with his left foot, he then spun around and struck an acrobatic shot with his right. *2–0!*

'That's more like it!' Casemiro thought to himself, and in the final moments of the match, he almost added a brilliant third for Brazil. When Gabriel slid the ball across to him on the edge of the area, he struck it first time, sending a curling shot flying towards the top corner... but no, it bounced back off the crossbar!

So unlucky! Oh well, Brazil had the win they needed, and there would be plenty more opportunities for Casemiro to become a national hero...

With Neymar Jr out injured, Brazil found it even harder to break through and score in their second match against Switzerland. Raphinha, Richarlison and Vinicius all had good chances, but none of them could grab that all-important goal. Oh well, were they going to have to settle for a disappointing draw?

No, in the eighty-third minute, Brazil's big-game player decided it was time to step forward. Casemiro drifted into the box from deep, and when the ball dropped to him, he took his chance brilliantly. In a flash, he smashed a spinning shot into the far corner of the net. *1–0!*

Goooooooooooooooooooooaaaaaaaaaaaaaaaallllllllllllll llllllllllll!!!!!!!!!!!!!!!!!!!!!!

Job done! Casemiro jogged over to the corner flag like it was no big deal, but of course it was – he had just become Brazil's World Cup hero!

What would the national team do without him? Once the match was won, Neymar Jr posted a message on social media: 'Casemiro has been the best midfielder in the world for a long time.'

Wow, his old friend hadn't said 'best *defensive* midfielder'; he'd said 'best midfielder'. That really was high praise indeed!

With Brazil already through to the knockout stages, Tite rested Casemiro for the final group game against Cameroon, and the result? They lost! Never mind, he was back for the match that really mattered: the Round of 16 clash with South Korea. Although as it turned out, there wasn't much dirty work for their defensive midfielder to do...

Vinicius Jr calmly fired a shot past four defenders

and the keeper. *1–0!*

Neymar Jr scored from the penalty spot. *2–0!*

Richarlison finished off a beautiful, flowing team move. *3–0!*

Lucas Paquetá made a late run into the box and guided the ball in on the volley. *4–0!*

Woah, what a fantastic first-half performance! Brazil were sending a powerful message to the other teams at the tournament: 'Watch out, we're here to win this World Cup!'

Next up, in the quarter-finals: Croatia, captained by Casemiro's great friend, Luka. But while it was lovely to share a football pitch with each other again, they were both fully focused on leading their countries to victory.

Vamooooosssssssssssss!

Playing against a strong Croatia defence, sadly it was like the Switzerland game all over again, only this time, it took Brazil even longer to score. But at last, at the end of the first half of extra-time, Neymar Jr changed everything with a moment of magic. After a double one-two with Rodrygo and then Lucas, he dribbled around the goalkeeper and scored. *1–0!*

'Yessssssssssss!' Casemiro cried out, falling to his tired knees. Surely, that was it – the winning goal that took them through to the World Cup semi-finals?

But instead of staying back and holding on to their lead, Brazil kept attacking and searching for a second goal. So, when Luka managed to get the ball past Casemiro, it was four Croatia forwards against four defenders. Danger alert! Too late. Mislav Oršić crossed the ball to Bruno Petković, and his shot deflected off Marquinhos and flew past Alisson. *1–1!*

Noooooooooo! Casemiro couldn't believe it; after all their hard work, Brazil had thrown their lead away, and now the match was heading to penalties! Oh well, what was done was done; now, they would have to win the shoot-out to stay in the World Cup.

'I'll take one,' he told Tite with total confidence as usual. By the time he stepped up, Rodrygo's first spot-kick had already been saved, but Casemiro calmly guided his shot into the bottom corner. *GOAL!* With a quick fist-pump, he walked over to Alisson to wish him good luck.

Unfortunately, however, Croatia kept scoring, and

when Marquinhos hit the post, it was all over. Once again, Brazil had been beaten in the World Cup quarter-final.

NOOOOOOOOO! Casemiro stood there frozen on the halfway line for ages, with his hands on his hips and a horrible feeling in his stomach. How on earth had they lost that match? After so many years of winning, it was by far the most painful defeat of his football career.

CHAPTER 22

UPS AND DOWNS AS UNITED'S GUARD DOG

The only good news for Casemiro after that painful World Cup exit was that he didn't have too long to dwell on it. Two weeks later, he was back in action for Manchester United, doing what he did best: winning football matches.

Casemiro's main job was to be the guard dog in midfield, protecting the team from dangerous attacks. But the Brazilian could do a whole lot more than just defend:

Against Nottingham Forest, he raced forward to win the ball and then slid it across for Fred to score. *ASSIST!*

Against Bournemouth, he volleyed in from

Christian's free kick. *GOAL!*

In the Manchester Derby against City, he helped inspire an incredible comeback with a sweeping pass through to Bruno. *ASSIST!*

Yessssss, Case!

Three games, three wins – United were on fire and up into the Premier League Top Four! And that wasn't all; they had also made it all the way through to the EFL Cup final.

The chance to lift a trophy at Wembley? Casemiro couldn't wait. In the big game against Newcastle, he used all his big-game experience to lead his team to victory.

In the first half, Casemiro raced in between three defenders and powered a header into the bottom corner. *1–0!*

Goooooooooooooooooooooaaaaaaaaaaaaaaaaalllllllllllllll lllllllllllll!!!!!!!!!!!!!!!!!!!!

Then in the second half, with his team 2–0 up, Casemiro stayed back and kept things calm and organised in midfield, winning balls and playing simple passes, until the final whistle blew. Hurray,

Manchester United had won the 2023 EFL Cup!

'A magical day at Wembley,' Casemiro posted on social media afterwards. 'We are the Champions!'

He was so happy to have his first trophy already, but as the season went on, it wasn't all fun and goals for United's guard dog. Sometimes, he had dirty work to do in defence, and sometimes that dirty work got him into trouble.

Foul!

Free kick.

Come on, ref – you've got to book him for that!

Casemiro liked to do his research on the referee before every match he played – their background, their style, what they were especially strict on – but it didn't always work. Before long, he received his fifth yellow card of the season, which meant he had to miss their important Premier League match against Arsenal. And the result? United lost.

It was clear that the team needed their guard dog back, but in the very next game against Crystal Palace, Casemiro got involved in an argument and was given a red card. Nooooo, now he would have to miss another three matches!

And sadly, that wasn't the end of it. In his second game back against Southampton, Casemiro slid into a reckless tackle on Carlos Alcaraz and received another red card!

Noooo, not again – this was becoming a nightmare! Casemiro buried his face in his black gloves to hide his tears as he trudged slowly off the field.

What was going wrong? In nine years at Real Madrid, he had only been sent off twice, and now he had been sent off twice within his first season at United. Was it just bad luck, or did he have to change the way he played? One thing was for sure – the suspensions had to stop. His team needed him out there on the pitch, helping them to win.

When Casemiro finally returned in mid-April, there were only eight Premier League games to go. United were still in fourth place, the final Champions League spot, but Tottenham were only three points behind them, and Liverpool were catching up too…

'Right, let's do this!' Casemiro declared. Manchester United had lost their two best centre-backs, Raphaël and Lisandro Martínez, to injury, but now they had their midfield guard dog back, and he was determined to play in the Champions League next season. Plus, he wanted to make things right after those red cards.

So, Casemiro grabbed the winner against Bournemouth with a stunning scissor-kick. *GOAL!*

And he scored against Chelsea too, with a clever flick header. *GOAL!*

Hurray, United had secured a Champions League spot, and with a last win over Fulham, they even finished the season in third place. And that wasn't all; they were also off another trip to Wembley for the FA Cup final against Manchester City!

This time, Casemiro's big-game experience wasn't quite enough to lead his team to victory, but as his first year in England came to an end, he had plenty to feel proud about: fifty-one games, seven goals, seven assists, two cup finals, one trophy, plus Champions League football secured for next season. Not bad for a player who was supposedly 'past it'!

Casemiro wasn't someone who could just sit back and switch off over the summer, though. At Real

Madrid, the Brazilian had become a world-class winner, which meant that he always wanted more.

'I hear everyone saying that Manchester United is back, but this is only the beginning of our journey,' he wrote to the fans a few days later. 'Here, defeat is not acceptable, and the glory days must return. For that I have come. Come on, United!'

São Paulo

🏆 South American Cup: 2012

Real Madrid

🏆 Spanish League: 2016–17, 2019–20, 2021–22

🏆 Spanish Cup: 2013–14

🏆 Spanish Super Cup: 2017, 2019–20, 2021–22

🏆 UEFA Champions League: 2013–14, 2015–16, 2016–17, 2017–18, 2021–22

🏆 UEFA Super Cup: 2016, 2017, 2022

🏆 FIFA Club World Cup: 2016, 2017, 2018

Manchester United

🏆 EFL Cup: 2022–23

Brazil

🏆 South American U-17 Championship: 2009

🏆 South American U-20 Championship: 2011

🏆 FIFA U-20 World Cup: 2011

🏆 Copa América: 2019

Individual

🏆 UEFA Champions League Squad of the Season: 2016–17, 2017–18

🏆 Spanish League Team of the Season: 2019–20

🏆 Copa América Team of the Tournament: 2021

CASEMIRO

18 **THE FACTS**

NAME: Carlos
Henrique Casimiro

DATE OF BIRTH:
23 February 1992

AGE: 31

PLACE OF BIRTH:
São José dos Campos

NATIONALITY: Brazil

BEST FRIEND: Luka Modrić
and Toni Kroos

CURRENT CLUB: Manchester United

POSITION: DM

THE STATS

Height (cm):	185
Club appearances:	554
Club goals:	54
Club trophies:	20
International appearances:	71
International goals:	7
International trophies:	1
Ballon d'Ors:	0

★ ★ ★ **HERO RATING: 87** ★ ★ ★

GREATEST MOMENTS

20 AUGUST 2011,
BRAZIL 3–2 PORTUGAL

Casemiro was already a breakout star for his club, São Paulo, but this Under-20 World Cup win was when he first became a hero for his country. Although he didn't grab any goals at the tournament, Casemiro did get one assist, and he was the reliable rock at the centre of the Brazil team.

28 MAY 2016, REAL MADRID 1–1 ATLÉTICO MADRID (REAL WON ON PENALTIES!)

For the 2014 Champions League final, Casemiro hadn't even made the Real Madrid bench, but two years on, he was now one of the first names on Zinedine Zidane's teamsheet. Playing alongside Luka Modrić and Toni Kroos in midfield, Casemiro did an incredible job of protecting the defence and this time, he was able to celebrate properly because he had played a key part in the victory.

3 JUNE 2017, REAL MADRID 4–1 JUVENTUS

Okay, so Casemiro's shot took a massive deflection, but who cares about that? He certainly didn't. He had scored a crucial goal in a major final to lead his team towards their second Champions League trophy in a row. A year later, Real Madrid would make it three in a row, with Casemiro at the heart of the midfield again.

2 JULY 2019, BRAZIL 2–0 ARGENTINA

After their early exit at the 2018 World Cup, Casemiro was desperate to bring joy to Brazil again by winning the 2019 Copa América. His performances were heroic throughout the tournament, but in this semi-final against Argentina, he was at his ball-winning best, battling away to keep Lionel Messi quiet. It worked, and after beating Peru in the final, the trophy was theirs.

26 FEBRUARY 2023, MANCHESTER UNITED 2–0 NEWCASTLE UNITED

Within his first six months in England, Casemiro had already helped his new club to reach the EFL Cup final. And in the big game at Wembley, he used his big-game experience to lead Manchester United to the trophy. Not only did he score the first goal of the game, but he also controlled the midfield brilliantly, and collected the Man of the Match award too. What a winner!

TEST YOUR KNOWLEDGE

QUESTIONS

1. Which family member helped get Casemiro into his first-ever football team?

2. What disease did Casemiro get during his early days at the São Paulo academy?

3. How old was Casemiro when he first visited Manchester United's Old Trafford stadium?

4. True or false – Casemiro won the FIFA U-20 World Cup with Neymar Jr?

5. Which Real Madrid manager handed Casemiro his first-team debut in 2013?

6. In 2014, Casemiro spent one very important season at which other European club?

7. Which Real Madrid manager made Casemiro his main man in midfield in 2016?

8. What nickname did Carlo Ancelotti give to his amazing midfield trio: Casemiro, Luka Modrić and Toni Kroos?

9. Which two Manchester United players helped persuade Casemiro to join the club?

10. Casemiro scored his first goal for Manchester United against which Premier League team?

11. How many red cards did Casemiro receive during his first season at Manchester United?

Answers below . . . No cheating!

1. *His cousin Monica.* 2. *Hepatitis.* 3. *Fifteen.*
4. *False! Neymar Jr wasn't part of Brazil's squad.* 5. *José Mourinho.*
6. *Porto.* 7. *Zinedine Zidane.* 8. *The Bermuda Triangle.*
9. *Fred and Raphaël Varane.* 10. *Chelsea.* 11. *Two.*

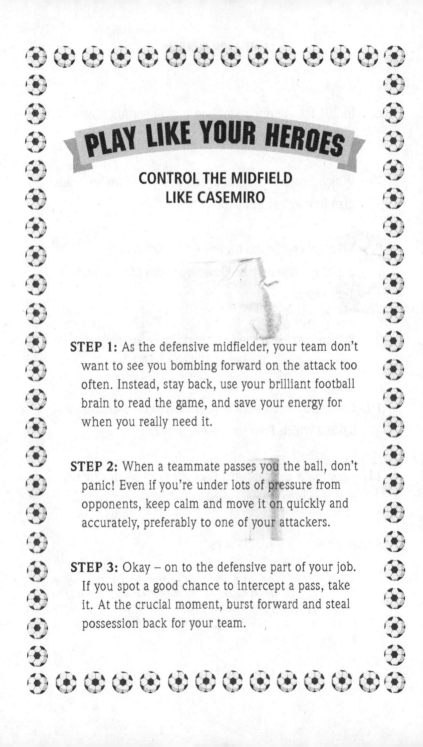

PLAY LIKE YOUR HEROES

CONTROL THE MIDFIELD
LIKE CASEMIRO

STEP 1: As the defensive midfielder, your team don't want to see you bombing forward on the attack too often. Instead, stay back, use your brilliant football brain to read the game, and save your energy for when you really need it.

STEP 2: When a teammate passes you the ball, don't panic! Even if you're under lots of pressure from opponents, keep calm and move it on quickly and accurately, preferably to one of your attackers.

STEP 3: Okay – on to the defensive part of your job. If you spot a good chance to intercept a pass, take it. At the crucial moment, burst forward and steal possession back for your team.

STEP 4: If you notice that one of your defenders is out of position, drop back and help out. You're there to protect the team, and you might even get a 'Thanks!' or a high-five for your efforts.

STEP 5: If the other team launches a quick counter-attack, it's your job to stop them. Blocks, headers, tackles – do whatever it takes to win the battle. The aim is always to win the ball fairly, but if you don't, never mind – it's probably a good foul to give away. They don't call it dirty work for nothing!

STEP 6: But just because you're a defensive midfielder, it doesn't mean you can't ever go forward and grab the glory. You just need to pick your moments carefully, like going up for corners and free kicks, or making powerful late runs into the box.

CAN'T GET ENOUGH OF
ULTIMATE FOOTBALL
HEROES?

Check out heroesfootball.com
for quizzes, games, and competitions!

Plus join the Ultimate Football Heroes
Fan Club to score exclusive content and
be the first to hear about
new books and events.
heroesfootball.com/subscribe/